MONNA VANNA

A PLAY IN THREE ACTS

BY

MAURICE MAETERLINCK

TRANSLATED BY

ALEXIS IRÉNÉE DU PONT COLEMAN

NEW YORK AND LONDON

HARPER & BROTHERS

CAST OF CHARACTERS

GUIDO COLONNA . . . *Commander of the garrison of Pisa.*

MARCO COLONNA . . . *Father of Guido.*

PRINZIVALLE . . . . *Captain in the service of Florence.*

TRIVULZIO . . . . . *Commissary of the Republic of Florence.*

BORSO . . . . . . *Lieutenant to Guido.*

TORELLO . . . . . *Lieutenant to Guido.*

VEDIO . . . . . . *Secretary to Prinzivalle.*

VANNA . . . . . . *Wife of Guido.*

Nobles, soldiers, peasants, men and women of the city, etc.

SCENE.—Acts I. and III., at Pisa; Act II., in the camp outside the walls.

TIME.—End of the fifteenth century.

MONNA VANNA

ACT I

SCENE.—*A hall in the palace of* GUIDO
COLONNA. *Discovered:* GUIDO *and his
lieutenants,* BORSO *and* TORELLO, *near
an open window, from which a view is
gained of the country about Pisa.*

GUIDO

HE extremity to which we
are reduced has forced the
Council to confess disas-
ters that they have long
hidden from me. The two
armies sent to our aid by
Venice are themselves besieged by the
Florentines, one at Bibbiena, the other at
Elci. The passes of the Vernia, of Chiusi
and Montalone, Arezzo, and all the defiles
of the Casentine are in the hands of the
enemy. We are cut off from the whole

world, given over defenceless to the wrath
of Florence, that pardons only when she
fears. Our bands and the populace are yet
ignorant of these defeats; but rumors fly
among them, more and more disquieting.
What will they do when they shall know
the truth? Their anger and their despair-
ing terrors shall fall upon us and upon the
Council. They are stirred to the verge of
madness by three months of siege, of famine,
and of hardships the like of which scarce
a city hath ever borne. The only hope
that still held them submissive despite their
sore trouble is about to crumble before their
eyes—and then there is naught but revolt,
the insweeping of the foe, and so an end of
Pisa!

BORSO

My men have nothing left—not an arrow,
not a bullet; and you shall search every tun
in the vaults without finding an ounce of
powder.

TORELLO

It is two days since I fired our last shot
against the batteries of San Antonio and

the tower of Stampace. Now that naught
is left them but their swords, even the
Stradiotes refuse to go upon the ramparts.

BORSO

You may see from hence the breach that
Prinzivalle's cannon have made in the walls
our Venetian allies were defending. It is
fifty ells in width—a flock of sheep might
pass through it with ease. No man can
make a stand there; and the foot-soldiers
from the east, the Slavonians and Albanians,
swear that they will all desert if we do not
sign the capitulation this night.

GUIDO

Three times in these ten days the Council has sent elders from the college to
treat of terms — and we have seen them
no more.

TORELLO

Prinzivalle cannot pardon us the death of
his lieutenant, Antonio Reno, slain in our
streets by the furious peasants. Florence

[3]

draws her profit from it, to reckon us out-
laws and barbarians.

GUIDO

I sent my own father to tell and to excuse
the error of a maddened multitude whom
we could not contain.   He was sure a sacred
hostage—yet he is not returned.

BORSO

Now for a week past the town lies open
on every side, our walls are ruined, and our
cannon silent.   Why comes not Prinzivalle
to the assault?   Is it that his courage fails
him, or hath Florence sent dark and hidden
orders?

GUIDO

The orders of Florence are always dark,
but her designs are clear.   Too long has
Pisa been the faithful ally of Venice; it is
an evil example for the small towns of
Tuscany.   The Republic of Pisa must be
blotted from the earth.   Little by little,
cunningly and silently, they have poisoned
this war, provoking cruelties and unaccus-

tomed perfidy, that they may the better
justify the vengeance they will take. Not
without reason do I suspect their emissaries
of having goaded on our commons to murder
Reno. Nor is it idly that they have sent
against us the most savage of their hirelings,
the barbarous Prinzivalle—that same whose
exploits at the sack of Piacenza are so famous. There, after that he had slaughtered,
they said carelessly, all the armed men, he
put to sale as slaves five thousand free-born
women.

BORSO

They have erred that tell the tale. It
was not Prinzivalle, but the commissaries of
Florence that ordained both the slaughter
and the sale. I have never seen this Prinzivalle, but one of my brothers knew him.
He is of outlandish birth; his father was a
Basque or a Breton, it would seem, and had
set up as a goldsmith in Venice. He is of
low descent, in sooth, but not the savage
that men paint him. They call him violent,
heady, a loose liver, a dangerous foe, but

a man of honor. I would yield him my sword without fear. . . .

GUIDO

Yield it not so long as it may defend you. We shall see him at his work, and know then which of us two is in the right. Meantime we must essay the last chance of men who will not be slaughtered without so much as lifting an arm. First, we must needs tell the whole truth to the soldiers, the towns-men, and the peasants who have taken shelter with us. They must know that no terms are offered us—that it is no longer question of one of those peaceful wars when two great armies fight from dawn till dusk to leave three wounded men upon the field, one of those brotherly sieges where the con-queror becomes in a day the guest and the dearest friend of the vanquished. It is a struggle without quarter, in which life and death alone are face to face—in which our wives, our children . . . [*Enter* MARCO. GUIDO *catches sight of him and goes quickly to greet and embrace him.*] Father! . . .

[6]

By what happy chance, amid all our ills, by
what blessed miracle, have you come safe
back to us when I had ceased to hope? You
are not wounded? You walk painfully. . . .
Have they tortured you? Did you escape?
What have they done to you?

MARCO

Nothing, thank Heaven—they are not barbarians. They welcomed me as men welcome a guest whom they revere. Prinzivalle had read my works; he spoke to me
of the three dialogues of Plato that I found
and translated. If I halt in my walk, it
is because I am old, and I have come a long
way. Can you guess whom I met in Prinzivalle's tent?

GUIDO

I can hazard a guess—the merciless commissaries of Florence.

MARCO

Yes, in truth—them, too, or one of them,
for I saw but one. . . . But the first man
who was named to me there was Marsiglio

[7]

Ficino, the venerable master who revealed
Plato to my eyes—Marsiglio Ficino, the very
soul of Plato born again on earth! I would
have gladly given ten years of my life to see
him before I shall go the way of all flesh,
We were even as two brothers who meet
after a long absence. . . . We spoke of
Hesiod, of Aristotle, of Homer. . . . In an
olive-grove near the camp he had discovered, buried in the sand of the river-bank, the
torso of a goddess so strangely fair that if
you saw it you would forget the war. We
dug farther—he found an arm, and I un-
earthed two hands so pure and fine that one
would think them formed to call up smiles
by their caresses or to spread the gentle dew
of dawn. One of them was curved as slender
fingers are when they press a dainty breast,
the other still held the handle of a mirror . . .

GUIDO

Father, forget not that a people is dying
of hunger; there are other things for them
to think of than delicate hands and a bronze
torso.

[8]

MARCO

Marble, my son—it was of marble.

GUIDO

Be it so; let us rather speak of thirty thousand lives that may be lost by one imprudence, one moment of delay, or saved perchance by a wise word, by good tidings. It was not for a torso or a pair of severed hands that you went forth. What did they tell you? What will they do with us— Florence or Prinzivalle? Speak! What do they wait for? You hear those wretched souls that cry beneath our windows? They are struggling for the grass that grows between the stones. . . .

MARCO

True, I had forgotten that you are at war—now, when spring comes again, when the sky breathes of happiness like that of a king that wakes from his slumbers, when the sea swells like a cup of light that a shining goddess holds to her bright consort, when the earth is so fair and hath such love

[9]

for men!   But you have your joys—I speak
too long of mine.   Ay, you are right; I
should have told you straight the news I
bring.   It saves thirty thousand lives, to
sadden one; but it offers this one the noblest
of chances to cover itself with a glory that
seems higher to me than the glories of war.
Love for one sole object is happy and laud-
able; but love that rises to greater heights,
that seeks a wider range, is better.   Nay,
watchful purity and faith are excellent virtues; but there are times when they seem
but small if one look elsewhere.   So, then
. . . But fly not up at the first words, to cut
off your retreat by oaths that will bind you
when reason would turn back. . . .

GUIDO

[*Dismissing the officers by a sign.*]   Leave
us.

MARCO

Nay, remain.   It is our common fate that
we must decide.   *My* wish would be that
the hall were filled with all the victims we
are to save, that they listened at the win-

dows to grasp and hold fast the salvation I
bring—for I do bring rescue, if reason can accept it; though ten thousand reasons would
scarce outweigh a heavy error, one so heavy
that I fear its weight the more because I myself . . .

GUIDO

Leave these riddles, father. What can it
be that makes such demands on us? Surely
we are strong enough to hear all—and we
have reached the hour when nothing can
longer astonish us.

MARCO

Know, then, that I saw Prinzivalle and
spoke with him. How strangely we may be
deceived by the image of a man painted by
those who fear him! I went even as Priam
to the tent of Achilles. . . . I thought to
find some barbarian, arrogant and heavy,
always covered with blood or plunged in
drunken stupor; at best, the madman they
have told us of, whose spirit was lit up
at times, upon the battle-field, by dazzling
flashes of brilliance, coming no man knows

whence. I thought to meet the demon of combat, blind, unreasoning, vain and cruel, faithless and dissolute.

GUIDO

And such is Prinzivalle, only not faithless.

BORSO

True, he is honorable, even though he serve Florence; twice hath he proved it to us.

MARCO

Now I found a man who bowed before me as a loving disciple bows before the master. He is lettered, eager for knowledge, and obedient to the voice of wisdom. He will listen long and patiently, and has a feeling for all beauties. He loves not war; his smile speaks of understanding and gentle humanity. He seeks the reason of passions and events. He looks into his own heart; he is endowed with conscience and sincerity, and it is against his will that he serves a faithless state. The hazards of life, his destiny perchance, have turned him to the career of

arms and chain him still to a kind of glory
that he despises and would gladly leave;
but not before he has satisfied one desire—
a dark and terrible desire, such as come to
certain men who are born, it would seem,
under the fatal star of a single mighty love
that may never be realized. . . .

GUIDO

Father, you must not forget how long the
time is to men that perish of hunger. Let
us leave these qualities that concern us not,
and come to the word of salvation that you
promise us.

MARCO

It is true, . . . I may have unduly delayed it; and cruel as it is to the two whom
I love best on earth . . .

GUIDO

I take my part—but whose shall the other
be?

MARCO

Listen, and I will tell you. When I came
hither it seemed strange and difficult; but

on the other hand, the chance of salvation was so prodigious and unlooked for . . .

GUIDO

Speak!

MARCO

Florence is resolved to blot us out; the Council of War decrees it necessary, and the Signoria approves their judgment. There is no appeal. But Florence, always hypocritical and prudent, is loath to bear the blame of too bloody a triumph in the eyes of the world to which she is the apostle of civilization. She will maintain that Pisa refuses the terms of clemency offered by her. The town will be taken by assault, the Spanish and German bands let loose upon us. There will be no need to give them special orders when there is a prospect of pillage and rape and burning and massacre. It is enough to say that they pass beyond the restraining hand of their commanders—who will easily find themselves powerless on that day. Such is the fate they reserve for us; and the city of the

[14]

lilies, if the overthrow should prove more cruel even than she dares to hope, will be the first to deplore it, and to attribute it to the unforeseen license of the soldiery, which she will dismiss with signs of loathing after our ruin has made their help needless. . . .

GUIDO

I see Florence in all that.

MARCO

Such are the secret instructions transmitted to Prinzivalle by word of mouth from the commissaries of the Republic. This week past they have been pressing him to deliver the assault. He has delayed till now on divers pretexts. For his part, he has intercepted letters by which the commissaries, who watch his every movement, accuse him to the Council of treason. Pisa once destroyed and the war over, judgment, torture, and death await him in Florence, as they have awaited more than one captain who grew dangerous. Thus he knows his fate.

[15]

GUIDO

Good! What does he propose?

MARCO

He counts—as surely as a man may count on these changeable savages—on a certain part of the archers whom he enrolled himself. In any case, he is sure of a guard of a hundred men who will form a base for his plans, utterly devoted to him. He proposes, then, to bring into Pisa all that will follow him, to defend you against the army he abandons.

GUIDO

It is not men we lack—least of all such dangerous auxiliaries. Let them give us powder and ball and victuals. . . .

MARCO

Good! He foresaw that you would reject an offer that might well seem so doubtful. He will promise, then, to throw into the town a convoy of three hundred wagons laden with victuals and munitions that has but newly arrived in his camp.

GUIDO

How will he do it?

MARCO

I do not know—I understand nothing of
the ways of war and statecraft. But he
does as he will; despite the Florentine commissaries, he is sole master in his camp, so
long as the Council has not recalled him.
And it would not dare to recall him on the
eve of a victory, from the midst of an army
that has the prey all but in its grasp and
believes in him. They must wait their
time. . . .

GUIDO

So, then, I understand that he will save
us in order to save himself and to antici-
pate his vengeance. But he might do it in
a more striking or a more subtle manner.
What interest has he in loading his enemies
with favors? Where will he go—what will
become of him? What does he ask in exchange?

MARCO

Now comes the moment, son, when words

become cruel and mighty — when two or three of them suddenly put on the strength of fate and choose their victims! I tremble when I think that the sound of these words, the manner in which they are pronounced, may cause many a death or save many a life. . . .

GUIDO

I cannot fathom this. . . . The most cruel words can add nothing to real misfortunes.

MARCO

I have told you that Prinzivalle seems wise, that he is humane and reasonable. But where is the wise man that hath not his private madness, the good man to whom no monstrous idea has ever come? On one side is reason and pity and justice; on the other—ah! *there* is desire and passion and what you will — the insanity into which we all fall at times. I have fallen into it myself, and shall, belike, again—so have you. Man is made in that fashion. A grief which should not be within the experience of man is on the point of touching you; and I, who

see so clearly that it will be out of all pro-
portion to the evil that it answers to, have
made for my part a promise madder yet than
this grief, mad as that will be. Yet this
promise, in all its folly, shall be kept by the
wise man that I pretend to be, I that come
to speak to you in the name of reason. I
have promised, if you reject his offer, to return to the enemy's camp. What shall be-
fall me there? Torture and death will likely
be the reward of so absurd a loyalty; yet I
shall go. It is well enough to tell myself
that it is but a remnant of childish folly that
I am dressing up in purple; none the less I
shall commit the folly that I disdain, for I
have no longer the strength to follow my
reason. But still I have not told you. . . .
I am losing myself in a labyrinth of words, I
am piling up obstacles to keep from me the
decisive moment. . . . Yet it may be that
I am wrong to doubt of you. . . . Hearken:
this great convoy, the victuals that I have
seen, wagons running over with corn, others
full of wine and fruit; flocks of sheep and
herds of cattle, enough to feed a city for

months; all these tuns of powder and bars
of lead, with which you may vanquish
Florence and make Pisa lift her head—all
this will enter the city to-night, . . . if you
send in exchange, to give her up to Prinzivalle until to-morrow's dawn, . . . for he
will send her back when the first faint gray
shows in the sky, . . . only, he exacts that,
in sign of victory and submission, she shall
come alone, and her cloak for all her covering. . . .

GUIDO

Who?   Who shall thus come?

MARCO

Giovanna.

GUIDO

My wife?   Vanna?

MARCO

Ay, your Vanna.   I have said it!

GUIDO

But why my Vanna, if such are his desires?   There are a thousand women—

MARCO

Because she is the fairest, and . . . he loves her.

GUIDO

He loves her? Where can he have seen her?

MARCO

He has seen her and knows her—he would not say when or how.

GUIDO

But she—has she seen him? Where can he have crossed her path?

MARCO

She has never seen him—or so her memory tells.

GUIDO

How know you that?

MARCO

She herself told me.

GUIDO

When?

MARCO

Before I came to find you.

GUIDO

And you told her? . . .

MARCO

All.

GUIDO

All? What, all the infamous barter?
You could dare? . . .

MARCO

Ay.

GUIDO

And what said she?

MARCO

She answered nothing, but grew pale and
left me without a word.

GUIDO

Ay, so it pleases me best! She might
have leaped upon you, have spat in your
face, or fallen senseless at your feet. . . .

[22]

But I like it better that she but turned pale
and left you. So would an angel have done.
That is my Vanna. There was no need of
words. We, on our side, will say nothing.
We will take our post once more upon the
ramparts—if it be but to die, we die at least
without staining our defeat . . .

MARCO

My son, I understand you—and the trial is
wellnigh as harsh for me as for you. But the
blow has now been struck—let us give reason
time to put our duty and our pain in their
right places.

GUIDO

There can be but one duty in face of this
abominable offer — no reflection can do
aught but add to the horror it inspires.

MARCO

Yet ask yourself if you have the right to
give a whole city up to death, and but to
put off by some sad hours an inevitable ill.
When the city is taken, Vanna will be in the
victor's power. . . .

[23]

GUIDO

Nay, . . . leave that to me.

MARCO

So be it, . . . but these thousands of lives, say to yourself that they are much, . . . too much, perchance—and that it is not just. . . . If your own welfare were all that hung upon this choice, you might well choose death and I would approve you, even though I, nearing the end of a life that has seen many men and thus many human griefs, doubt the wisdom of preferring death with its cold horrors, its eternal silence, to any suffering in body or even in soul that may delay it. . . . But here it is a question of thousands of other lives—brothers in arms, women, little children. . . . Yield to this madman's demand, and what seems monstrous to you will be heroic to those who live after you and will look upon your act with a calmer and so a juster eye. Believe me, nothing is worth a life that one saves; all the virtues, all the ideals of man, all that he calls honor, fidelity, and the like, seem but a child's game in comparison. You would traverse a fearful trial as a hero— yet they err who believe that heroism has no other height but in death. The most heroic act is that which costs the most— and death is often less painful than life.

GUIDO

Can it be that you are my father?

MARCO

And proud of the name. If I strive against you to-day, I strive equally against myself, and should love you less did you yield too soon.

GUIDO

Ay, you are my father—you have proved it, for you, too, would choose death. Since I reject this abominable compact, you will return to the enemy's camp, there to suffer the fate that Florence decrees. . . .

MARCO

My son, there is no question here of a useless graybeard, who has but few days to

[25]

live and matters little to any one. Therefore it is that I tell myself it is waste of
time to combat an ancient folly in myself
and struggle to raise what I must do to the
height of wisdom. I do not know why I
shall go thither. . . . The soul in my old
body is still too young—I am far enough
yet from the age of reason. But, though
I deplore it, the force of the past prevents
me from violating a mad promise. . . .

GUIDO

I shall follow your example.

MARCO

What do you mean?

GUIDO

Like you, I shall be faithful to that power
of the past which seems absurd to you,
though, happily, it still rules your actions. . . .

MARCO

It rules me only when others come into
question. If your mind needs, for its en-

[26]

lightenment, the sacrifice of an old man's
word, I will give up the keeping of my
promise, and, do what you will, I will not
go back to them. . . .

GUIDO

Enough, father—or I shall speak words
to you that a son ought not to speak even
to an erring father.

MARCO

Say all the words that indignation calls
up in your heart—I shall take them only
as the evidences of a just grief. My love
for you does not depend on the words you
speak. But, though you curse me, let reason and benign pity come into your heart
to take the place of the harsh thoughts that
come from it. . . .

GUIDO

That will suffice—I cannot listen longer.
Reflect on what thing it is you would have
me do. It is you that are false to reason,
to any high and noble reason; the fear of

death troubles your accustomed wisdom.
As for me, I look upon this death with less
disquietude—I recall the lessons of courage
you gave me before age and the vain study
of many books enfeebled yours. No man
has witnessed your weakness save my two
officers, and they will keep with me the
secret that we shall not, alas! have long to
carry. Let it be buried in our breasts; and
now to speak of the final combat. . . .

MARCO

Nay, my son, it cannot be buried; my
years and my vain studies have taught me
that no man's life may thus be hidden from
sight. If you fancy that I have no longer
the only kind of courage that you honor,
there is another, less brilliant, it may be, and
less vaunted by men's tongues, since it does
less harm, and they venerate that by which
they suffer. . . . That will strengthen me to
accomplish what remains of my duty.

GUIDO

What is it that remains?

MARCO

I must finish what I have begun in vain.
You were one of the judges in this cause, but
not the only one; all those whose life and
death hangs in the balance have the right to
know their fate and its conditions. . . .

GUIDO

I do not clearly see—at least, I hope I do
not. You would say? . . .

MARCO

. . . That when I leave this room, it will be
to tell the people of Prinzivalle's offer, which
you reject.

GUIDO

Good—now, at least, I understand. I am
sorry that useless words have brought us
thus far, and that your strange madness
forces me to seem wanting in the respect due
to your age. But a son's duty is to protect
a mistaken father even against himself.
Moreover, while Pisa stands I am master
here and guardian of its honor. Borso and
Torello, I give my father into your charge.

You will guard him until his conscience shall
have come to itself.   Nothing has happened
—no one shall know.   Father, I pardon you
—and you will pardon me when the last hour
shall reawaken in you the memory of the
days when you taught me to be a man without fear or conscious weakness.

MARCO

My son, I pardon you before that last hour
comes.   I should have done like you.   You
may imprison me, but my secret is free—it
is too late already to stifle my voice.

GUIDO

What mean you?

MARCO

That in this very hour the Council is de-
liberating on the proposal of Prinzivalle.

GUIDO

The Council? . . . Who has told them?

MARCO

I—before I told you.

[30]

GUIDO

No! It is not possible that the fear of
death and the ravages of old age can so far
have unbalanced you that you would thus
give over my only happiness, all the love, all
the joy, and all the purity of both our lives,
to strange hands, who will coldly weigh and
measure them, as they weigh salt and measure oil in their shops! I cannot believe it—
I will not believe it until I have seen it.
But if I shall have seen it, ah! then I shall
look upon you, my poor old father that I
used to love, that I thought I knew, that I
tried to resemble a little, with as much horror as I should have for the obscene and cruel
monster who has plunged us into all this
misery!

MARCO

You speak truth, son, when you say you
have not known me well enough. . . . I accuse
myself of the fault. When my gray hairs
came to me, I did not share with you what
each day taught me of life and love and human happiness and misery. Often a man
may live thus, close to those he loves, and

not tell them the only things that count.
He goes on, cradled in the memory of the
past, believing that all other things are
transformed with him; and when misfortune
rouses him, he sees with horror how far they
have drifted the one from the other. If I
had told you sooner the changes time was
working in my heart, the vanities that were,
one by one, dropping from me, the realities
that were expanding in their place, I should
not now stand before you as an unhappy
stranger whom you are on the verge of
hating. . . .

GUIDO

I am happy in knowing you so late. For
the rest, naught avails. I know what the
Council will choose. It is too easy, for-
sooth, to save themselves thus at the cost of
a single man—it is a temptation which more
courageous souls than these merchants, who
would fain go back to their counters, could
not resist. But I do not owe them such a
sacrifice—to none do I owe it! I have given
them my blood, my sleepless nights, all the
toils and sufferings of this long siege—it is

enough. The rest is mine. I will not yield
—I will remember that I still command here.
There are at least my three hundred Stradiotes that will hear no voice but mine and
will take no part in the plots of cowards!

MARCO

My son, you are wrong. The Council of
Pisa, these merchants whom you despise
without knowing their decision, have given,
in the midst of their distress, an admirable example of noble firmness. They have refused
to receive their safety at the cost of a woman's purity and love. At the moment when
I left them to come to you, they were sum-
moning Monna Vanna to tell her that they
left the fate of the city in her hands.

GUIDO

What? They have dared? When I was
absent, they have been bold enough to re-
peat before her the evil words of that vil-
lanous satyr! My Vanna! When I think
of her delicate visage, to which a look would
bring the blush, where every pure thought

came and went unceasingly, as though to
refresh the splendor of her beauty. . . . My
Vanna before them—old men with shining
eyes; pale, paltry merchants with the smile
of hypocrites, that trembled before her as
before a holy thing. . . . They will have said
to her, "Go to him, even after the manner
of his demand." They would have her go
to yield up to him that body which no man
ever dared to think on with so much as a
passing breath of desire, so virginal did it
appear; from which I, her husband, ventured
not to draw the veils but with a charge to
my hands, my eyes, to keep perfect rever-
ence, lest I should sully it by one ill-gov-
erned thought. . . . And while I speak they
are there and say to her —! They are
noble and resolute, you tell me—they will
not force her to go without her will. What
will they do when I stand before them? They
only ask for her consent—but mine, who has
asked it?

MARCO

Have not I, my son? If I do not gain it,
they will come in their turn. . . .

GUIDO

There is no need for them to come—
Vanna will have answered for us both.

MARCO

I hope she may—if you will accept her
answer.

GUIDO

Her answer? Can you doubt of it? Yet
you know her—you have seen her day by
day, since that first hour when, covered with
the flowers and the smiles of her one love,
she crossed the threshold of this very hall to
which you come to sell her, where you doubt
of the answer, the only answer a woman can
make to a father who so forgets himself as to
ask that she . . .

MARCO

Every man, my son, sees in another that
which he knows in himself—and sees it in a
different fashion, reaching to the height of
his own conscience.

GUIDO

Ay, perchance that is why I knew you so

ill. . . . But if my eyes must be opened twice,
on two errors so cruel — God! I would far
rather close them forever.

MARCO

They would close, my son, but to open in
greater light. If I speak thus, it is that I
have seen in her a strength that you know
not, . . . so that I do not doubt of her answer. . . .

GUIDO

Nor will I doubt of it. I accept it here
and now, before I know it, blindly, firmly,
irrevocably. If it is not the same as mine,
it is that we have been deceived the one in
the other, from the first hour until this day
—that all our love has been one huge lie that
now falls asunder—that all I adored in her
had no existence save in this poor, credulous
brain, so near to madness, in this miserable
heart that knew but one happiness, and that
a phantom!

> [*The murmur of a throng is heard off.*
> *They repeat the name of* MONNA
> VANNA. *The door up stage opens,*

and VANNA, *alone and very pale,*
advances into the room, while the
crowd of men and women press tim-
idly about the threshold, as though
not daring to enter, and wishing to
conceal their presence. GUIDO, *see-*
ing her, goes swiftly to her, takes her
hands in his, caresses her face, and
kisses it with feverish ardor.

My Vanna! What have they done to
you? Nay, nay, tell me not the things they
have said! Let me look upon your face and
deep down within your eyes. . . . Ah! all is
still as pure and clear as the pools in which
angels bathe. They could not sully what I
loved; all their words have fallen only as
stones thrown into the air, that fall back
without troubling for an instant the serene
clearness of the azure heaven. When they
looked upon these eyes, they dared to ask
no question, or they found their answer
written there—the clearness of your glance
set a great lake of light and love between
their thoughts and yours. But now look;

come hither. . . . There stands a man I call
my father. . . . See, he bows his head—the
white locks fall about it to hide his face!
You must pardon him—he is old and wandering. . . . Have pity on him—recall him by
your words; your eyes are not enough, so far
is he from us. He knows us no longer—our
love has passed above his blind old age as an
April shower above a barren rock. He has
never caught one of its rays, never surprised
the meaning of a single one of our kisses.
He must have words to understand your
answer—tell him your answer!

VANNA

[*Approaches* MARCO.] Father, I will go to-
night.

MARCO

[*Kisses her forehead.*] I knew, daughter . . .

GUIDO

Ha! What is that? Are your words for
him or for me?

VANNA

For you, too, Guido. I shall obey. . . .

[38]

GUIDO

But whom? All lies in that. I know not
yet. . . .

VANNA

I go to-night to Prinzivalle's camp. . . .

GUIDO

To give yourself to him according to his
demand?

VANNA

Even so.

GUIDO

To die with him? To kill him first? I
had not thought. . . . Say that, and I shall
understand!

VANNA

I shall not kill him—the city would be
sacked. . . .

GUIDO

What? And is this *you?* Then you love
him—you have loved him? Say how long!

VANNA

I do not know him—I have never seen
him.

GUIDO

But you know what manner of man he is? They have spoken of him . . . have told you . . .

VANNA

One said he was an old man—I know no more. . . .

GUIDO

He is not old. He is young and handsome —younger than I. . . . Why has he asked this one thing? I would have gone to him on my knees, my hands bound, to save the city. I would have gone from here alone, alone and penniless with her, to be a wanderer to the end, and beg my bread on desolate highways. . . . But this foul dream of a barbarian! . . . Never, in any age or in any story, has a conqueror dared— . . . [*Approaches* VANNA *and embraces her.*] Vanna! My Vanna! I cannot believe it yet—it is not your voice that speaks. . . . I have heard nothing, all is as it was. It was my father's voice thrown back by the walls. Tell me that I have heard wrong—that all our love, all your purity said *no*, cried aloud *no*, since

the shame of such a choice was forced upon
you! I heard nothing, tell me, but a be-
lated echo; . . . it is the unbroken silence that
you are now to part. All listen eagerly—
none knows anything—the first word is yet
to come from you. Speak it swiftly, Vanna,
that they may know you as you are—speak
it swiftly to scatter an evil dream and to
proclaim the greatness of our love! Speak
the word for which I wait, the word I need
to sustain all that is tottering and ready to
fall to ruin in me! . . .

VANNA

Well I know, Guido, that your part of the
burden is the heaviest. . . .

GUIDO

[*Instinctively repelling her.*] I bear it alone!
He who loves carries all the burden. And
you never loved me. . . . Such things cost
little to those who have no heart. . . . It is
something new—perchance even a joy. . . .
Ah! but I shall know how to spoil that joy!
Let men say and do what they please, I am

still master here! And what would you say
if I rose up against this horror, if I shut you
in my good prison—oh, a chaste prison, dungeons cool and fresh, that lie beneath this
hall—with my Stradiotes to watch every
door, until your warmth died down and
your heroism were a shade less ardent? [*To
the officers*.] Take her! I have spoken—
the order is given. Obey me!

VANNA

Guido, you know well . . .

GUIDO

They obey not? No one moves? Borso,
Torello, are your arms turned to stone? Can
you hear my voice no longer? And you,
yonder, that listen at the door, does it reach
your ears? I will cry so loud that the very
rocks shall fly apart! Enter, seize her, all
the world has leave! . . . I see—they are
afraid—they desire to live. . . . They shall
live, then, while I die. . . . God! it is too easy!
One man alone against the throng—one that
pays the debt of all. . . . Yet why should I

be that one? You all have wives. . . . [*He
half draws his sword and approaches* VANNA.]
And what if I preferred your death to the
shame of both of us? You had no thought
of that. . . . Ay, but look! . . . One stroke,
and it is done! . . .

VANNA

You will do it, Guido, if love commands
you. . . .

GUIDO

Love! *You* to speak of love, that you
have never known! Nay, it is true—you
have never loved. I see you now as you are
—drier than a sandy desert that has swal-
lowed up my all! Not a tear. . . . I was nothing to you but a shelter you had need of. . . .
If for a moment . . .

VANNA

Look, Guido, I cannot speak. . . . Look in
my face. . . . My strength fails me. . . . I am
dying. . . .

GUIDO

[*Takes her passionately in his arms.*] Come

[43]

to my arms, Vanna! It is there that you
will live!

VANNA

[*Repulses him, her body becoming rigid.*]
No, no, no, no, Guido! I know. . . . I cannot
speak. . . . All my strength fails me if I say
one word. . . . I cannot. . . . I would only—
I have reflected well. . . . I know. . . . I love
you, I owe all to you. . . . I may be vile and
abandoned — and yet I must go — I must
go. . . .

GUIDO

[*Thrusts her from him.*] It is well. . . . Go,
go, leave me—go to him. I yield all. Go
to him— I cast you off. . . .

VANNA

[*Seizes his hands.*] Guido . . .

GUIDO

[*Repulsing her.*] Ah, do not cling to me
with your soft, warm hands! My father
was right; he knew you better than I. See,
father—there is your work. Finish it to the
very end. Lead her to his tent. I will stay

[44]

here and see you go. But think not that I
shall take my share of the food she is to buy.
One thing is left to me — soon you shall
know. . . .

VANNA

[*Clings to him.*] Look at me, Guido! Do
not hide your eyes. . . . That is the only
threat. . . . Look at me. . . . I must see . . .

GUIDO

[*Looks at her and repulses her more coldly.*]
See, then. . . . Go—I know you no more.
The time draws near—he is waiting—night
falls. Fear nothing. . . . Are my eyes the
eyes of a man who will do acts of madness?
One does not die thus when love has melted
away into nothingness—it is while love reigns
that reason totters. . . . Mine is firm now.
. . . I have seen love to its very depths—love
and purity. . . . There is no more to say.
Nay, unlace your fingers—they cannot hold
love that departs. It is all over—not a trace
remains. All the past has sunk into the abyss
—and all that was to come. . . . There was a
time when I believed. . . . but all is over!

[45]

[*Frees himself from both of* VANNA'S *hands.*]
There is nothing now. . . . less than nothing.
. . . Farewell, Vanna — go — farewell. . . .
You will go to him? . . .

VANNA

I shall go. . . .

GUIDO

You will not return? . . .

VANNA

Yes, . . . if . . .

GUIDO

We shall see. . . . Ah! good; . . . we shall
see. . . . Who would have thought that my
father knew her better than I?

> [*He staggers and supports himself
> against one of the marble pillars.*
> VANNA *exits slowly, alone, without
> looking at him.*

CURTAIN

ACT II

SCENE.—*The tent of* PRINZIVALLE. *Sumptuous disorder. Hangings of silk embroidered in gold. Arms, costly skins, large coffers half open, full of jewels and splendid stuffs. Entrance to tent up stage, overhung with tapestry. Discovered:* PRINZIVALLE *standing near a table, on which he is arranging parchments, plans, and arms. To him enter* VEDIO.

VEDIO

 ERE is a letter from the commissary of the Republic.

PRINZIVALLE

From Trivulzio?

VEDIO

Yes—Messer Maladura, the second commissary, is not yet returned.

[47]

PRINZIVALLE

It must be that the Venetian army which
threatens Florence through the Casentine is
not so easily vanquished as they had hoped.
Give me the letter. [*Takes the letter and
reads it.*] It brings me for the last time,
under pain of immediate arrest, the order in
all the forms to attempt the assault at day-
break. Well, the night is mine. . . . Immediate arrest! They have no suspicion. . . .
They imagine that they can still terrify, by
the aid of old, worn-out words, the man who
waits the supreme hour of his life. Threats,
arrest, trial, judgment, what else you will—
I know what it all means. Long ago they
would have arrested me if they had the
power, if they dared. . . .

VEDIO

Messer Trivulzio, when he gave me the
order, said that he would follow me to speak
with you.

PRINZIVALLE

He has at last made up his mind to that?
Then it will be decisive; the sorry little

scrivener, that stands for all the mysterious power of Florence here and dares not look me in the face, the white-faced, puny creature, that hates me worse than death, shall pass such a night as he has not foreseen! The orders must be grave, for him to affront the monster in his cage. . . . What guards are at my door?

VEDIO

Two old soldiers of your Galician troop—
I think I knew the features of Hernando;
the other is, I fancy, Diego. . . .

PRINZIVALLE

Good—they will obey me, did I ordain them to throw God the Father into chains. The day is fading. . . . Have the lamps lit. What is the hour?

VEDIO

Past nine.

PRINZIVALLE

Marco Colonna has not yet returned?

[49]

VEDIO

I gave orders to the watch to bring him to
you as soon as he crossed the moat.

PRINZIVALLE

He was to be here before nine if they re-
jected my offer. . . . This is the hour that tells
the tale ; . . . it holds my life within it, like
the mighty ships with all sails spread that
the prisoners shut within a bubble of glass,
together with their hopes and dreams. . . .
How strange it is that a man can place his
destiny, his heart and mind, his happiness
or woe, on so frail a thing as a woman's love!
. . . I should laugh at it myself, if it were not
a thing beyond my laughter.   Marco returns
not. . . . It must be that she is coming. Go
see if the beacon that should say *yes* is there
—the light in the heavens that heralds the
trembling steps of her that gives herself for
all, and comes to save me and her people at
once. . . . Nay, I will go myself.   No other
eyes, even a friend's, must see it before mine,
must delay one moment the joy to which I
have looked from boyhood. . . . [*Goes to door*

[50]

of tent, raises the tapestry, and looks out into the night.] Lo, Vedio, the light! See how it blazes out and dazzles the night! It was the campanile that should bear it—see, it leans out over the shadows. No other light shows in the town. Ah! Pisa has never raised aloft a more splendid ensign—never one more desired or less hoped for! Ah, my good Pisans! to-night you shall celebrate an hour never to be forgotten, and I shall have greater joy than had I saved the city of my birth!

VEDIO

[*Seizes his arm.*] Let us go within the tent —yonder comes Messer Trivulzio.

PRINZIVALLE

[*Comes down.*] True—there is yet need. . . The conference shall be brief. [*Goes to table and turns over the papers.*] You have his three letters?

VEDIO

There were but two.

[51]

PRINZIVALLE

The two that I seized, and this evening's order.

VEDIO

Here are the two first—and here the last; but you have marred it. . .

PRINZIVALLE

I hear him. . . .

[*A guard raises the curtain. Enter* TRI-
VULZIO.

TRIVULZIO

Have you remarked the unaccustomed light that burns in signal from the campanile?

PRINZIVALLE

You take it for a signal?

TRIVULZIO

Not a doubt of it. . . . I have somewhat to say to you, Prinzivalle.

PRINZIVALLE

I hear. Leave us, Vedio—but go not far I shall have need of you. [*Exit* VEDIO.

TRIVULZIO

You know, Prinzivalle, the esteem in which I hold you. I have given you more than one proof of it that you cannot have forgotten—but there are others of which you are ignorant; for the policy of Florence, that men call perfidious while it is but prudent, requires many things to remain hidden for a time, even from those who are most in her counsels. We all obey her deep-laid plans, and each man must bear with courage the weight of the mysteries that make the strength of his country. Let it suffice you to know that I have ever had my part in the decisions that have raised you step by step, despite your youth and your unknown origin, to the command of the Republic's finest armies. There has been no reason to regret our choice; yet, for some time past, a party has been taking shape against you. I am not so sure whether the real friendship I have formed for you does not, in revealing these plots, trench a little on my strict duty; . . . but strict duty is often more harmful than the most wanton generosity. I will con-

fide to you, then, that men speak bitterly
of your delays and hesitations—some even
go so far as to doubt your honor. Precise
accusations have come to confirm their suspicions. They have made an evil impres-
sion on that part of the Council which was
already ill - disposed to favor you. They
went so far as to deliberate on the question
of arresting and judging you. By good fort-
une, they warned me first. I betook myself
to Florence, and it was not hard to oppose
proofs as good to their proofs. I answered
for you—and it is your turn now to justify my
confidence, which has never admitted a single
doubt—for we are lost if you do not act.
My colleague, Messer Maladura, is held in
check at Bibbiena by the troops of Venice;
another army marches on Florence from the
north. The very safety of the city is at
stake. All may be repaired if to-morrow
you deliver the attack so long awaited.
'Twill give us back our best army, and the
only captain whom victory has always
crowned; it will permit us to enter Florence
with our heads high, in the midst of a triumph

[54]

such as shall render your enemies of yesterday your most fervent admirers and parti-
sans. . . .

PRINZIVALLE

You have said all yo' can.? to say?

TRIVULZIO

Nearly—though I have said little of the
sincere affection which since I first knew you
has but grown stronger in me, . . . despite the
difficulties into which we are led by the con-
flict of our laws, which provide that the gen-
eral's power shall be balanced, in moments
of peril, by the mysterious might of Florence,
. . . whose humble proctor I am to-day, amid
all the splendor and the clash of arms. . . .

PRINZIVALLE

This order, that I have but now received,
is from your hand?

TRIVULZIO

It is.

PRINZIVALLE

The writing is your own?

TRIVULZIO

Undoubtedly—do you question it?

PRINZIVALLE

And these two letters—do you acknowl-
edge them?

TRIVULZIO

It may be. . . . I know not. . . . What do
they contain? That I should first know. . . .

PRINZIVALLE

There is no need—*I* know!

TRIVULZIO

They are the two letters you intercepted,
as I meant you should?   I see the test was
good.

PRINZIVALLE

You had not to do with a child.   Let us
have an end of these miserable shifts, and
not prolong a meeting that I am in haste to
finish, that I may receive a recompense such
as no Florentine triumph could ever equal.
In these same letters you denounce all my
acts, basely, falsely, without avowable mo-

[56]

tive, for the sole pleasure of injuring another, and to furnish in advance the pretext
indispensable to the thankless avarice of
Florence, that fears once again lest her reward to a victorious soldier cost her too dear.
All is travestied there with so treacherous
a skill that there were moments when I
doubted of my own innocence! All is de-
formed, poisoned, abased by your weak and
purblind envy, by your bitter hate—from
the first week of the siege until the day, the
happy day, when at last I have opened my
eyes, and am at last about to justify your
suspicions. I copied your letters with care;
I sent them to Florence, and I surprised
the answers. They take you at your word
—the more readily as they themselves fur-
nished you with the theme of your accusations. They judge me unheard, and con-
demn me to death already. After that, I
know that were I clothed in the innocence
of archangels I should not escape from the
proofs that are to overwhelm me. Therefore, at a bound, I break your paltry chains,
and I attack the first. Hitherto I have been

[57]

no traitor; but since these letters I have prepared your ruin. This night I shall sell you,
you and your sorry masters, as cruelly and
as finally as I may. I shall think that never
in my life have I accomplished an act more
salutary than in thus abasing, to the utmost
of my power, the only state that places perfidy in the number of its civic virtues, and
wills that hypocrisy, ingratitude, villany, and
falsehood shall govern the world! This
evening, by my act, your ancient foe, that
hinders and will hinder you while she lives
from leaving your own walls to corrupt the
world—this night Pisa shall be saved and
shall rise to brave you once again. Do not
spring up and make useless gestures. My
measures are taken—it is the inevitable.
You are in my power—and, as I hold you,
so methinks I hold the destinies of Florence. . . .

TRIVULZIO

[*Draws his dagger and strikes rapidly at him.*]
Not yet—while my hands are free! . . .

       [PRINZIVALLE *parries the stroke in-
           stinctively with his arm, and thus*

[58]

strikes up the blade so that it scratch-es his face. He seizes TRIVULZIO *by the wrist.*

PRINZIVALLE

Ah! . . . I did not think of your convulsive terror. . . . But now you are in my hands— and you feel that one of them is stronger than your whole body. Here is your dagger, now. I have but to turn it downward. . . . It seems of its own free will to seek your throat. . . . Not a quiver of your eyelids— you have no fear?

TRIVULZIO

[*Coldly.*] No—strike! It is your right. I staked my life. . . .

PRINZIVALLE

[*Loosens his hold.*] Truly? . . . Then your act is curious and even rare. There are not so many among our rude warriors that would have thrown themselves thus into the very jaws of death—I would not have believed that in this frail body . . .

[59]

TRIVULZIO

You that have always the sword in your hand are too much given to believing that there is no other courage than that which shines from its point. . . .

PRINZIVALLE

You may be right. . . . Good! You are not free, but no harm shall come to you. We serve different gods, that is all. . . . [*Wipes the blood from his face.*] Ah, I am bleeding—the stroke was a shrewd one; a little over-hasty, but vigorous. 'Twas near enough, on my word! Tell me, now, what would you do if you held in your power a man who had been so near sending you on the instant to a world where no one longs to go?

TRIVULZIO

I would not spare him.

PRINZIVALLE

I cannot fathom you—you are a strange being. Confess that your letters were base. . . . I had shed my blood in three great bat-

tles; I was doing my utmost; all was yours;
I served loyally those who had made choice
of me, without a single dishonest thought
in my heart. You must know that, since
you spied upon me. . . . And yet in your letters, were it from hatred, from envy, or to
save a few gold pieces, you gave a false color
to all the deeds that were done to save your
cause; you lied knowingly—you heaped lie
upon lie. . . .

TRIVULZIO

It matters little that what I wrote was
false. It was my task to seize the dangerous hour when the soldier, puffed up with
two or three victories—the number varies
little—is about to disobey the masters who
employ him—those who have a higher mission in the world than his. This hour proves
that the other was near. The populace of
Florence love you too much already—it is
our task to remove the idols they set up.
They look askance at us for the moment—
but they have created us to cross their per-
ilous caprices for them. They know their
end in life better than might be supposed,

and when we destroy what they have adored
too long, they feel that we do but accomplish their own will in spite of them. So I
knew that the hour had come to warn Florence of its idol; it knew what my lies
meant. . . .

PRINZIVALLE

The hour had not come — would never
have come if your hideous letters . . .

TRIVULZIO

It might have come—that was enough for
me.

PRINZIVALLE

What! An innocent man sacrificed on a
mere suspicion, without regret, to avert a
danger that in a certain case might possibly
have been a real one! . . .

TRIVULZIO

One man weighs but little in the scale,
with Florence in the other.

PRINZIVALLE

Then you believe in the destiny of Flor-

ence—in her work, in her life? She means
something to you that I cannot understand.

TRIVULZIO

I believe only in her—the rest is nothing
to me.

PRINZIVALLE

After all, it is possible. . . . And you are
right, since you believe in it. I have no
country. . . . I cannot know. . . . It seems to
me at times that I should have had one. . . .
But I have all else that you will never have
—that no man has had in such full measure.
. . . I shall have it here—now—in a moment.
. . . This is enough to make up for all!
Come, let us break off—we have not the
time to balance these enigmas. Every man
has his destiny; one has an idea, and another
a desire. And it would cost you as much to
change your idea as me to change my desire.
We follow them to the end, when we have a
stronger soul than the multitude—and that
which we do is just, since we have so little free-
dom to choose. . . . Farewell, Trivulzio—our
ways lead asunder. . . . Give me your hand.

TRIVULZIO

Not yet. . . . I will offer you mine in the
day when judgment . . .

PRINZIVALLE

So be it.   You lose to-day—you will win
to-morrow.   [*Calls.*]   Vedio!

[*Re-enter* VEDIO.

VEDIO

What, master!   You are wounded?   The
blood flows. . . .

PRINZIVALLE

It is a trifle.   Call my two guards.   Let
them take this man away without ill-treat-
ing him. . . . He is a foe that I love.   They
will put him in a sure place, and let no man
see.   I hold them to account for him; they
are to yield him up only when I give order.

[*Exit* VEDIO, *taking* TRIVULZIO *with
him.* PRINZIVALLE *goes to mirror
and examines his wound.*

I bleed as if the wound were mortal. . . .
It is not deep, but the half of my face *is*

torn. Who would have believed that so
white and frail a creature . . . ? [*Re-enter*
VEDIO.] 'Tis done?

VEDIO

Ay — but, master, you go that way to
your ruin.

PRINZIVALLE

That way? I would go that way to my
death! Never a man since the world began
will have thus gained, in a just vengeance,
the only joy he has dreamed since he knew
how to dream at all! I would have waited
and watched for it, and pursued it through
all the crimes, for it was mine by right; and
now that my good star sends it down to me
upon its silver rays, in the name of justice,
in the name of pity, you say to yourself,
"He goes to his ruin!" Poor creatures without a spark of the divine flame, men without
love! Why, you do not know that at this
hour my destiny is being weighed in heaven,
that they are piling up there what should
have gone to make a hundred joys, for
a thousand lovers! Ah, *I* know! I am at

5   [65]

the point where those who are born to a noble triumph or a great disaster find themselves suddenly on the very pinnacle of their lives, where everything upholds them, everything balances them there, everything gives itself to them! And what is that which follows to them? We know that man is not made for such triumphs, and that those who gain them sink under their weight, . . . but . . .

VEDIO

[*Approaches, with white linen.*] The blood still flows. . . . Let me bandage your face.

PRINZIVALLE

Well, since it must be. . . . But see that your linen does not cover my eyes or enfold my lips. . . . [*Looks at himself in the mirror.*] Ah! I am more like a wounded man that flees the surgeon than a lover that will soon leap to meet his love. Not so, Vedio, . . . not so. . . . And you, my poor Vedio, what will become of you?

VEDIO

Master, I follow you.

PRINZIVALLE

Nay — leave me, rather. I know not where I shall go or what shall be my fate. You may escape — no man will pursue you; whereas with your master . . . I have gold in these coffers; . . . take it — it is yours. I have no more need of it. The wagons are harnessed, the flocks gathered?

VEDIO

You may see them from the tent-door.

PRINZIVALLE

Good! When I give the signal, do what is to be done. [*A shot heard off at some distance.*] What is that?

VEDIO

They are firing on the outposts.

PRINZIVALLE

Who gave the order? It must have been mistaken. . . . If it should be on *her!* . . . You warned them?

VEDIO

Ay; . . . it is impossible. I have posted guards that will lead her to you when she appears. . . .

PRINZIVALLE

Go and see.

> [*Exit* VEDIO. PRINZIVALLE *remains alone a moment. Then* VEDIO *re-enters, raises the tapestry over the door of the tent, and says in a low voice, "Master!" Then he retires, and* MONNA VANNA, *closely wrapped in a long cloak, appears and stops in entrance.* PRINZIVALLE *trembles violently, then takes a step towards her.*

VANNA

[*In a choked voice.*] I come as you have willed. . . .

PRINZIVALLE

There is blood on your hand! You are wounded?

VANNA

A bullet grazed my shoulder. . . .

PRINZIVALLE

When? Where? This is horrible!

VANNA

As I drew near the camp.

PRINZIVALLE

But who dared to fire? . . .

VANNA

I do not know—the man fled.

PRINZIVALLE

Show me the wound.

VANNA

[*Opening the upper part of cloak.*] It is here. . . .

PRINZIVALLE

Above the left breast. . . . It has not penetrated—the skin alone is touched. . . . Are you in pain ?

VANNA

No.

[69]

PRINZIVALLE

Will you let me have it dressed?

VANNA

No.

[*Pause.*

PRINZIVALLE

You are decided? . . .

VANNA

Yes.

PRINZIVALLE

Need I recall the terms of the . . .

VANNA

It is useless—I know them.

PRINZIVALLE

You do not regret? . . .

VANNA

Was it in the bond that I should come without regret?

PRINZIVALLE

Your lord consents?

[70]

VANNA

Yes.

PRINZIVALLE

It is my mind to leave you free. . . . There
is yet time, should you desire to renounce. . . .

VANNA

No.

PRINZIVALLE

Why have you done this?

VANNA

Because they were dying of hunger, and
would have died more speedily to-morrow.

PRINZIVALLE

No other reason?

VANNA

What other could there be?

PRINZIVALLE

I know that a virtuous woman . . .

VANNA

Yes . . .

PRINZIVALLE

One that loves her husband . . . with
all her heart . . .

VANNA

Yes . . .

PRINZIVALLE

You have put off your garments, all but
this cloak?

VANNA

Yes.

> [*Makes a gesture as if to prove it by
> throwing open the cloak.* PRINZI-
> VALLE *stops her by a sign.*

PRINZIVALLE

You have seen the wagons and the herds
ranged before the tent?

VANNA

Yes.

PRINZIVALLE

There are two hundred wagons filled with
the best grain of Tuscany; two hundred

more that bear forage for the beasts; fruit
and wine from the country of Sienna; thirty
more of powder brought from Germany, and
fifteen lesser ones of lead.   Near them stand
six hundred Apulian cattle, and twice as
many sheep.   All these await but your word
to go on their way to Pisa.   Would you see
them go?

VANNA

Yes.

PRINZIVALLE

Come to the tent-door.

> [*He raises the curtain, gives an order,
> and waves his hand.   A deep, con-
> fused noise begins.   Torches are lit
> and waved about, whips crack, the
> wagons begin to move, the animals
> utter their various cries and are set
> in motion.   *VANNA *and *PRINZI-
> VALLE, *standing in the tent-door,
> watch the huge convoy going off by
> torchlight into the starry night.*

From this hour, thanks to you, Pisa shall
go hungry no more.   She regains her might

and to-morrow she shall sing with the joy
and the glory of a triumph that no man
hoped for. Is that enough for you?

VANNA

Yes.

PRINZIVALLE

Let us close the curtains—give me your
hand. The evening has been pleasant, but
the night grows cold. You have come un-
armed, with no hidden poison?

VANNA

I have but my sandals and this cloak.
Strip me of all if you fear treachery.

PRINZIVALLE

It is not for myself that I fear, but for
you.

VANNA

I count not these things as more than
their lives.

PRINZIVALLE

That is well—you are right. Come and
rest a little. This is a soldier's couch, rough

J 74]

and hard, narrow as the grave, and little
worthy of you. Rest here, upon these skins
of aurochs and of great rams that do not
know yet how soft and precious a thing a
woman's body is. Place beneath your head
this gentler cushion — it is a lynx's skin,
given me by an African king on a night of
victory. [VANNA *sits, closely wrapped in her
cloak.*] The brightness of the lamp falls in
your eyes—shall I remove it?

VANNA

It matters little.

PRINZIVALLE

[*Kneels at foot of couch and seizes her hand.*]
Giovanna! [VANNA *raises her head, startled,
and looks at him.*] Oh, Vanna—my Vanna!
Yes, I, too, have been accustomed so to
call you; but now I have scarce strength to
speak the name. It has been so long a time
shut a prisoner in my heart that it can no
more issue without rending its prison. Nay,
it *is* my heart—I have no other! Each of
its syllables holds my whole life; when I

speak them, it is my life that flows away. It was familiar to me; I thought I knew it; I was no longer afraid of it when I had so often said it. For years past, every hour of every day, I have repeated it as some mighty word of love, some spell that one must some day have courage to pronounce at last, were it but once, in the presence of her whom it summoned in vain. . . . I believed that my lips had taken the shape of it, that at the supreme moment they would know how to say it with such sweetness and respect, with so humble and profound a meekness, that she who heard it would understand all the love and all the pain it held for me. But to-night it calls up no more than a shadow. It is no longer the same. I do not know it when it issues from my mouth, broken with sobs and tremulous with tears. I have put too much within it; all the emotion, all the adoration that I have imprisoned there break my strength, and my voice dies away. . . .

VANNA

Who are you?

[76]

PRINZIVALLE

You do not know me? . . . You recall nothing? Ah, how time effaces miracles! But
I was the only one that saw them. . . . Perchance it is better that they should be forgotten. . . . I shall have no more hope—I
shall the less regret. Nay, I am nothing to
you. I am but a poor wretch whose eyes
rest for one moment on the goal of his whole
life. I am an unhappy man that asks nothing, that knows not even what he should ask,
but who longs to tell you, if the thing is possible, that you may know before you leave
him, what you have been—ay! shall be to
the end in his life.

VANNA

You know me, then? Who are you?

PRINZIVALLE

You have never seen the man who gazes
on you, as one might gaze, in an enchanted
world, on the source of all his joy and of his
very life, . . . as I had never hoped to look
upon you?

VANNA

No; . . . at least I do not think so.

PRINZIVALLE

True, you did not know—I was sure, alas!
that you knew no longer. You were eight
years old, and I was twelve, when I crossed
your path for the first time. . . .

VANNA

Where was that?

PRINZIVALLE

At Venice; . . . it was a Sunday in June.
My father, the old goldsmith, brought a col-
lar of pearls to your lady mother. While
she admired them, I strayed into the garden.
. . . There I found you, under the myrtles,
near a fountain of marble. A tiny, golden
ring had fallen into the water—you were
weeping on the brink. I plunged into the
water and went near to drown, . . . but I
grasped the ring, and placed it again upon
your finger. You kissed me and were happy. . . .

VANNA

That was a fair-haired boy named Gianello. . . . You are Gianello?

PRINZIVALLE

I am he.

VANNA

Who would have known you?   And then your face is hidden by these bandages.   I can only see your eyes.

PRINZIVALLE

[*Pushes the bandages aside.*] Do you know me when I remove them?

VANNA

Yes—perhaps—methinks—for you have still a boy's smile.   But you are wounded, too, and bleeding. . . .

PRINZIVALLE

Ah, that is nothing to me.   But for you it is horrible. . . .

VANNA

The blood stains through everything. . . .

[79]

Let me set this bandage — it was ill tied.
[*She readjusts the bandage.*]   I have often
tended the wounded in this war. . . . Yes, I
bethink me. . . . I see again the garden, with
its pomegranates, its laurels, and its roses.
We played there more than one afternoon,
when the earth was warm and sunny. . . .

PRINZIVALLE

Twelve times. . . . I kept count. . . . I
could tell you all our games, and every word
of yours. . . .

VANNA

Then one day I looked for you . . . for I
loved you well. . . . You were grave and ten-
der as a girl, and you looked up at me as
though I were a young queen. . . . But you
did not come. . . .

PRINZIVALLE

My father took me with him when he went
to Africa. . . . We lost ourselves in those far-
off deserts.   I was a prisoner of the Arabs,
of the Turks, of the Spaniards, of whom you
will. . . . When I came back to Venice, your

[80]

mother was dead and the garden lay waste.
I lost all trace of you—then I found it again,
thanks to your beauty, which left an inef-
faceable memory wherever it passed. . . .

VANNA

You knew me on the instant when I came
in hither?

PRINZIVALLE

Had there come ten thousand of you into
my tent, all clad alike, all equally fair, ten
thousand sisters whom even their mother
would not know apart, I should have risen,
should have taken your hand, and said,
"This is she!" Is it not strange that a be-
loved image can live thus in a man's heart?
For yours lived so in mine that each day it
changed as in real life—the image of to-day
replaced that of yesterday — it blossomed
out, it became always fairer; and the years
adorned it with all that they add to a child
that grows in grace and beauty. But when
I saw you again, it seemed to me at first that
my eyes deceived me. My memories were
so fair and so fond—but they had been too

6 [81]

slow and too timid—they had not dared to
give you all the splendor which appeared so
suddenly to dazzle me.   I was as a man that
recalled to mind a flower he had but seen in
passing through a garden on a gray day, and
should be suddenly confronted with a hundred thousand as fair in a field bathed with
sunshine.   I saw once more your hair, your
brow, your eyes, and I found all the soul of
the face I had adored—but how its beauty
shames that which I had treasured in silence
through endless days, through years whose
only light was a memory that had taken
too long a road and found itself outshone
by the reality!

VANNA

Yes; you loved me as boys can love; but
time and absence deck love in flattering
colors. . . .

PRINZIVALLE

Men often say they have but one love in
their life—and it is seldom true. . . . They
trick out their desire or their indifference
with the marvellous unhappiness that be-
longs to those who are created for this single

love. When one of these, speaking the same words that are but a lie upon the lips of the others, comes to tell the profound and grievous truth that ravages his life, lo! the words too often used by happy lovers have lost all their force, all their weight; and she who hears them unthinkingly rates the poor words, so sacred and often so sad, at their profane value, in the smiling sense that they have among other men. . . .

VANNA

I shall not do that. I know what is this love that we all wait for when we set out in life, but renounce when the years . . . though my years are not so many! . . . dull the bright vision. But when, after you had passed through Venice, you came again upon the trace of me, what befell? You did not seek to stand in the presence of her you loved so much?

PRINZIVALLE

At Venice they told me that your mother had died in poverty, and that you married a great lord of Tuscany, the richest and most

powerful man of Pisa, who should make of
you a worshipped and happy queen. I had
naught to offer you but the wandering misery of an adventurer without a country or a
home. Methought that destiny demanded
of my love the sacrifice I made. I have
roved many a time near this city, lingering
beneath its walls, clinging to the chains of its
gates that I might not succumb to the desire
of seeing you, might not trouble the joy and
love that you had found. . . . I sold my
sword. I made two or three wars; my name
grew famous among mercenary captains. I
waited days and days, hoping no longer,
until the hour that Florence sent me to
Pisa. . . .

VANNA

How weak and cowardly men are when
they love! . . . Do not deceive yourself. I
have no love for you, and I dare not even
say that I had. But it makes the very soul
of love start and cry out within me when I
see a man that loved me as it might have
been that I loved him without courage in
presence of his love!

PRINZIVALLE

Courage I had—it needed more than you believe not to seek to see you. . . . But it was too late.

VANNA

It was not too late when you left Venice. It is never too late when one finds a love that fills the whole life. Such a love never abandons its hold; when it looks for no reward, it hopes yet. Though it should not even hope, it strives none the less. If I had loved like you, I would have—. . . Ah, one cannot say what one would have done! . . . But I know that Fate should not have snatched my hope from me without a struggle. I would have pursued it day and night. I would have said to Destiny, "Stand from out my path!" I would have summoned the very stones to take my part; and it would have needed that he whom I loved himself knew and pronounced my sentence—ay, pronounced it more than once!

PRINZIVALLE

[*His hand seeking hers.*] You do not love him, Vanna?

[85]

VANNA

Whom?

PRINZIVALLE

Guido? . . .

VANNA

[*Withdraws her hand.*] You must not seek my hand—I do not give it. I see that my words should be clearer. When Guido took me to wife, I was alone and poor, and a woman in such a state—above all, if she is beautiful and cannot stoop to easy lies—becomes the prey of a thousand calumnies. But Guido cared not—he had faith in me, and his faith pleased my heart. He has made me happy—as happy as one may be that has renounced the dreams a little wild that seem not made for our life here below. And you, too, will see—I can almost say I hope it—that a man may be happy without passing all his days in waiting for a joy such as none has ever known. . . . I love Guido with a love less wonderful, it may be, than that which you have thought to have, but more equal, constant, and sure. This is the

[86]

love that Fate has given me. I shall know
no other; and if it is broken, it will not be
by my hand. You have erred. If I have
found words that express your error, it was
not for myself nor for you that I spoke thus;
it was in the name of a love that the heart
sees in vision at the dawn of life, that exists,
perhaps, but is not mine, . . . and is not yours,
since you have not done what such a love
would have done. . . .

PRINZIVALLE

You judge me harshly, Vanna, without
sufficient knowledge of all that I have suffered, all that I have had to do, to bring
about this wonderful hour that would make
the despair of all other loves. Yet if my
love had done nothing, attempted nothing, I
know still that it exists, I who am its victim,
I who carry it within my breast, I whose
very life it devours, taking away all that
makes the glory and the joy of men. Since
it came upon me, I have taken no step whose
purpose was not to bring me nearer its goal,
to question my destiny without harm to you.

Ah, you may believe me, Vanna—men will believe those who hope nothing and ask nothing. . . . I have but to speak one word, to stretch out my arms, and I possess all that a common love may possess. But methinks you know as well as I that the love of which I speak has need of another sort of satisfaction. Therefore, I pray you to doubt no longer. This hand that I took, because I thought you would believe me, I shall touch it not again, neither with lips nor fingers. But, at least, Vanna, when we part forever, I would have you convinced that this love has been always yours, and has halted only before the impossible.

VANNA

It is because anything has seemed impossible to it that I venture still to doubt of it. Think not I should have rejoiced to see you surmount fearful obstacles, nor that I demand superhuman proofs. . . . They tell the story that one day in Pisa a maiden threw her glove into the lions' den, behind the campanile, and prayed her lover to go seek it

[88]

there.   He had no other arms than a leath-
ern whip; yet he leaped down, drove the
lions aside, took up the glove, knelt and gave
it her, and departed forever without a word.
Methinks he was too gentle.   His whip was
in his hand; he should have used it to teach
her that could so play with a divine thing
more of the rights and duties of true love.
I do not ask, then, that you shall furnish me
such proofs—I ask nothing better than to
believe you.   Yet it is for your welfare and
my own alike that I am forced to doubt. . . .
There is in a single-hearted devotion like
yours something sacred that must disquiet
the coldest and most virtuous of women. . . .
Therefore, I examine what you have done,
and should be wellnigh happy to find nothing there that bore the sign of this great
passion so rarely blessed. . . . I should be almost sure not to find it there, if your last act
—in that you have cast into the abyss your
past, your future, your glory, your life, only
to bring me for an hour to your tent—did
not force me to say that it may be you are
right. . . .

[89]

PRINZIVALLE

This last act is the only one that proves nothing.

VANNA

How can that be?

PRINZIVALLE

I would rather tell you the truth. . . . When I made you come hither, to save Pisa in your name, I sacrificed nothing. . . .

VANNA

I cannot understand. . . . You have not betrayed your country? You have not destroyed your past? You have not condemned yourself to exile, perchance to death?

PRINZIVALLE

For the first, I have no country. If I had, I do not think I should have sold it for my love, whatever that love had been. I am but a hired soldier, faithful to those who keep faith with him, but who betrays when he finds himself betrayed. . . . I have been falsely accused by the commissaries of Florence, condemned without a trial by a commonwealth of merchants—you know their ways as well as I do. I knew that I was lost. What I have done this night, far from being my ruin, may save me—if any chance can yet save me.

VANNA

Then you sacrificed no great thing?

PRINZIVALLE

Nothing. I owed it you to tell you. It would displease me to buy a single one of your smiles by falsehood.

VANNA

That is well, Gianello; that is worth more than love and its most triumphant proofs. You shall not need to seek the hand that shrank from you; . . . it is here. . . .

PRINZIVALLE

Ah! it would have given me more joy if love had won it for me. . . . But what matters it, since, after all, I hold it, Vanna? I gaze upon its ivory whiteness, I breathe its life, I drink in for a moment the sweet intoxication of an illusion—I clasp its warm freshness—see, I take it and stretch it out or close it at my will, as though it would answer me in the secret, magic tongue of lovers. I cover it with kisses, and you do not withdraw it. . . . You are not angry with me for putting you to this cruel test? . . .

VANNA

I should have done the same thing—a little better or a little worse—had I been in your place.

PRINZIVALLE

But when you yielded to come to my tent, you knew that I was . . . ?

VANNA

No one knew. There were strange-enough stories of the leader of our foes. Some would have you a horrible old man; others, a young prince of wonderful beauty. . . .

PRINZIVALLE

But Guido's father—he had seen me; did
he tell you naught?

VANNA

Not a word.

PRINZIVALLE

You did not ask him?

VANNA

No.

PRINZIVALLE

Then, when you came thus, at night,
defenceless, to give yourself into the
hands of an unknown barbarian, did not
your fair body tremble, your heart stand
still with fear?

VANNA

No—there was no help for it.

PRINZIVALLE

And when you saw me, you did not hesi-
tate?

[93]

VANNA

You have forgotten? I saw nothing at
first—these bandages . . .

PRINZIVALLE

Ay, but afterwards, Vanna, when I put
them aside? . . .

VANNA

That was another thing — and I knew
then. . . . But you — when you saw me
enter your tent, what was your design?
Did you mean in truth to abuse our pitiable
distress to the end?

PRINZIVALLE

Ah! I knew not too well what I meant to
do. I felt that I was lost—and I desired to
drag with me all I could. . . . And I hated
you, because of the love. . . . Yes, I should
have gone to the end had it not been *you*. . . .
Yet any other would have seemed odious to
me—you yourself would have had to be
other than you are. . . . I lose my reason
when I think of it. . . . One word would have
been enough that was different from your

[94]

words—one gesture that was not yours—
the slightest thing would have inflamed
my hate and let loose the monster. But
when I saw you, I saw in that same moment
that it was impossible.

VANNA

I saw it likewise, and I feared no longer;
... we understood each other without need
of words. It is strange. ... I think I should
have done even as you if I had loved as you.
... It seems to me at times that I am in your
place, that it is you that listen and I that
speak what you have spoken. ...

PRINZIVALLE

I, too, Vanna, from the first moment I felt
that the wall which shuts us off, alas! from
all other creatures grew transparent—that I
plunged my hands, that I bathed my eyes
in it as in a clear brook—that I drew them
out again and streams of light flowed from
them, streams of confidence and sincerity.
Methought that men were somehow changed
—that I had been deceived in their true nat-

ure until this day. . . . Above all, I thought
that I myself was other than of old—that I
emerged at last from a long imprisonment
—the doors were parted, flowers and green
leaves took the place of iron bars, the
sky stooped and drew up to it all the
heavy stones that had shut me in, and
the pure air of morning penetrated at last
into my heart and bathed my love in its
fresh fragrance. . . .

VANNA

I felt a change, too. . . . I marvelled that
I could speak to you as I have spoken since
the first moment. . . . I am silent by nature—
I have never spoken thus to any man, unless
it be to Marco, Guido's father. . . . And even
with him it is not the same. He has a thousand dreams that take up all his mind, . . .
and we have talked but a few times. The
others have always a desire in their eyes that
will not suffer one to tell them that one loves
them and would fain know what they have
in their hearts. In your eyes, too, a longing
burns; but it is not the same—it does not

affright me nor fill me with loathing. I felt
at once that I knew you before I remem-
bered that I had ever seen you. . . .

PRINZIVALLE

Could you have found it in your heart to
love me if my evil destiny had not brought
me back too late?

VANNA

If I told you that I could have loved you,
would not that be to love you now, Gianello?
And you know, as I know, that such a thing
may not be. But we are parleying here as
though we were in a desert island. . . . If I
were alone in the world, there would be
other things to say. But we forget too soon
all that another suffers while we are here,
smiling over the past. When I left the gates
of Pisa, the grief of Guido, the anguish of his
voice, the pallor of his face— . . . I can wait
no longer! The dawn must be near, and I
am eager to know. . . . But I hear steps; . . .
some one brushes the tent; and chance itself has more heart than we. They whis-

7 [97]

per at the entrance. . . . Hark! hark!
What is it?

> [*Hasty steps and low voices are heard
> outside the tent ; then* VEDIO'S *voice
> heard off.*

VEDIO

Master! . . .

PRINZIVALLE

It is Vedio's voice.   Enter!   What brings
you?

> [VEDIO *appears in door of tent.*

VEDIO

I have run hither. . . . Master, fly!   It is
time now. . . . Messer Maladura, the second
commissary—

PRINZIVALLE

He was at Bibbiena. . . .

VEDIO

He has returned. . . . He brings six hundred men — they are Florentines — I saw

them pass. . . . The camp is in a ferment. . . .
He brings orders—proclaims you traitor. . . .
He seeks Trivulzio. . . . I fear lest he may
find him before you can. . . .

PRINZIVALLE

Come, Vanna. . . .

VANNA

Whither?

PRINZIVALLE

Vedio, with two trusty men, shall lead
you back to Pisa.

VANNA

And you—whither will you go?

PRINZIVALLE

I know not yet—the world is wide enough
to offer me a refuge.

VEDIO

Master, have a care! They hold all the
country-side around—and all Tuscany is full
of spies. . . .

VANNA

Come to Pisa.

PRINZIVALLE

With you?

VANNA

Yes.

PRINZIVALLE

I cannot.

VANNA

If only for a few days. . . . Thus you would
escape the first pursuit. . . .

PRINZIVALLE

And your husband? . . .

VANNA

He knows the laws of hospitality as well
as you.

PRINZIVALLE

He will believe you when you tell him? . . .

VANNA

Yes. . . . If he did not believe me— . . .
But that is not possible.   Come.

[100]

PRINZIVALLE

Nay. . . .

VANNA

Why?   What do you fear?

PRINZIVALLE

It is for you that I fear.

VANNA

For me the danger is the same whether I
go alone or you are with me.   It is you that
should fear.   You have saved Pisa—'tis but
just if she save you.   You come beneath my
guardianship—I will answer for you.

PRINZIVALLE

I will go.

VANNA

That is the best proof your love could give
me.   Come. . . .

PRINZIVALLE

But your wound? . . .

VANNA

Yours is far graver.

[101]

PRINZIVALLE

Think not of mine—it is not the first.
But yours—it would seem that the blood . . .
[*Puts out his hand as if to throw aside
her cloak.*

VANNA

[*Checks him and gathers it more closely
about her.*] No, no, Gianello . . . we are enemies no longer. . . . I am cold.

PRINZIVALLE

Ah! I had half forgotten that you are but
thinly clad to brave the night air—and I am
the barbarian that has brought it so. But
yonder are the coffers in which I laid for you
the booty of the war. Here are robes of
gold, mantles of brocade. . . .

VANNA

[*Catches up some veils at random and wraps
them about her.*] Nay, these will suffice. I am
in haste to save you. Come, throw back
the curtains of the tent. . . .

[PRINZIVALLE, *followed by* VANNA,

[102]

*goes to the entrance and throws back
curtains. A confused noise, over all
of which is heard a sound of distant
bells, breaks the silence of the night.
Through the undulating curtains of
the tent Pisa is seen on the horizon,
all illuminated, with occasional fire-
works, making a great spot of brightness amid the night which is still
dark.*

PRINZIVALLE

Look, Vanna!—look!

VANNA

What is it, Gianello? Ah, I see! They
are the bonfires lit to celebrate your work.
The walls are covered with them, the ramparts flame, the campanile blazes like a joyous torch! All the towers throw answering
splendors back at the stars! The streets are
lanes of brightness in the sky. . . . I know
their outlines; I can follow them as clearly
as when by day I trod their stones. . . . There
is the Piazza with its fiery dome—and the

Campo Santo like an island of shadow. Life,
which seemed gone forever, comes quickly
back, shoots up the spires, rebounds from
the stones, overflows the walls and floods the
country-side—comes to meet us and to lead
us home. Hearken!... Do you not hear the
cries, the wild joy that mounts and mounts
as if the sea were flooding into Pisa—and the
bells sing out as on my marriage morn? Ah!
I am too happy before this joy that I owe to
him who has loved me best of all! Come,
my Gianello! [*Kisses him on the forehead.*]
That is the only kiss I may give you. . . .

PRINZIVALLE

Ah, my Giovanna! It passes the fairest
that my love had hoped! . . . But what is
this? You falter—your knees tremble. . . .
Come, lean on me; throw your arm about
my neck. . . .

VANNA

It is nothing. . . . I will follow you. . . . I
asked too much from a mere woman's
strength. . . . Support me, carry me, if need

[104]

be, that nothing may delay our first happy steps. . . . Ah, how fair the night is—and the dawn will soon be here! Hasten—it is time. . . . We must enter before the joy has faded. . . .

> [*They exit. his arm about her.*

CURTAIN

ACT III

SCENE.—*A hall of state in the palace of* GUIDO COLONNA. *Lofty windows, marble columns, porticos, canopies, etc. Up right a great terrace, whose balustrades bear huge vases full of flowers; to it leads up a double staircase outside. In centre, between the columns, large marble steps lead up to the same terrace, from which a view over the city is supposed to be afforded. At rise of curtain, enter* GUIDO, MARCO, BORSO, *and* TORELLO.

GUIDO

I HAVE done as you willed, as she willed, the will of all; now it is my turn. I have kept silence, effaced myself, held my breath, as a coward does when thieves are ransacking the house. And I have been

[107]

honest in my abasement! You have made a
scrupulous merchant out of me! See, yonder
is the dawn. . . . I have not moved till now.
I have weighed and counted the infamy. It
was needful to do honor to the bargain, and
to pay the price of the food you eat—to give
the buyer the last moments of this noble
night! Ah, the price was not too heavy for
so much corn, so many oxen. . . . Now I have
paid the price, and you have eaten, I am
free. Once more I am the master, and I
issue from my shame. . . .

MARCO

I know not what you would do, my son,
and none has the right to stand in the path
of a grief like yours. Nor can any soothe
it; the boundless happiness that springs from
it, that surrounds you on every side, I know
well can only render your first tears more
burning. . . . Now that the city is saved, we
go nigh to regret the safety that has cost so
dear—in our own despite, we bow our heads
in the presence of him who alone, unjustly,
bears the penalty. And yet, if yesterday

could return, I must still act as I acted then,
mark out the same victims, and urge the
same injustice; for the man who would be
just can do no more than pass his life in the
choice between two or three evils, which is
the greater. . . . I know not what words to
speak; but if my voice, once loved, can
penetrate once more the heart that always
listened to it, I would beg of you, my son,
not to follow blindly the first counsels of
your misfortune and your wrath. Await at
least the passing of the hour that makes
us speak irrevocable words. Vanna will return. . . . Judge her not to-day—repulse no
suppliant—do nothing that cannot be recalled. All that a man does under the press-
ure of too great a grief is so naturally and so
cruelly irreparable! Vanna will return, de-
spairing, yet happy. . . . See her not on her
return if you do not feel the strength to
speak to her as you would have done had
she returned a week ago from some absence.
For us poor mortals, the sport of so many
greater forces, there is so much virtue, so
much wisdom and justice, in the passing of

[109]

a few hours. The only words that count,
the words that we should look to when
misfortune blinds us, are those which we
shall speak after we have understood all, and
pardoned and love once more. . . .

GUIDO

Is that all? Here is an end! It is no
longer the hour of honeyed words, and there
is no one now whom they can deceive. Once
more I have stood by while you said what
you had to say to me—I was curious to
know what your wisdom had to offer me in
exchange for my life that it has so skilfully
destroyed. And this is what it gives me!
To wait, to have patience, to accept, to forget, to pardon, and to weep! No—it is too
poor an exchange! I had rather not be wise.
I must have more than words to lift me from
my shame. What I am about to do is simple—a few years back and you would have
laid it upon me. There is a man who has
taken Vanna from me—Vanna is no longer
mine while this man lives. I follow other
rules than those of the grammars. I obey

the great law that governs every man who
has a living heart in his breast. . . . Pisa has
store of arms and victual. I will have my
part of the arms. From this day her soldiers
belong to me—the best of them, those that I
enlisted and paid from my own purse. I owe
her nothing, and I claim what is mine. They
will come back to her only after they shall
have done what I demand of them in my
turn. For the rest, . . . Vanna I pardon—or
I will pardon her when he shall be no more.
She was deceived—she erred fearfully, yet,
after all, heroically. There were those who
played for evil upon her charity and greatness of soul. It is well—all this may, I will
not say be forgotten, but recede so far into
the distance of the past that even the love
that seeks it may not be able to find it. But
there is one that I shall never see without
shame and loathing. There is here a man
whose only mission was to be the guide and
the stay of a great and noble happiness,
and he became its enemy and its ruin. You
shall see a horrible thing, yet just—a son
who, in a world turned upside down, judges

his own father, curses him, denies him,
drives him from his presence, despises him,
and hates him!

MARCO

You shall curse me, my son, if you do but
pardon her. If in your eyes that has been
an unpardonable fault which has saved so
many lives, the fault is mine, the heroism
that of others. . . . My counsel was good;
yet it was easy, since I took no part in the
sacrifice. Now that it robs me of all I held
most dear, it wears a better aspect. You
have judged according to your lights, . . . as
I should have judged were I younger. . . . I
go, my son; you will see me no more. I can
understand that the sight of me is more than
you are able to bear; but I shall hope to see
you again when you shall not see me. . . .
Since I go without daring to hope that I shall
live to see the hour when you will pardon me
the wrong I have done you—for I have lived
long enough to know that forgiveness is slow
to those who, like you, are in the mid-course
of life—since I go thus, leaving nothing that

any man can envy me, let me at least be sure
that I bear with me all the hatred, all the
bitterness, all the cruel memories of your
heart—that none remain for her when she
returns. . . . I make but one prayer to you.
. . . Let me see her once more throw herself
into your arms—then I will go without a
murmur, without calling you unjust. It is
well that amid the tide of human misery the
old shall take upon their shoulders all that
they can bear—they have but a few more
steps to take before they are eased of their
burden. . . .

> [*During* MARCO'S *last words a great,
> confused noise has sprung up with-
> out. In the silence of the night it
> grows, draws nearer, and becomes
> more distinct. At first a mere mur-
> mur of expectation, it is heard soon
> to be composed of the acclamations of
> a multitude, distant at first, but draw-
> ing nearer. Then, through the vague
> uproar, cries are heard more and
> more   distinctly   of   "Vanna !"
> "Vanna !"   "Our Monna Van-*

na !" " Glory to Monna Vanna !"
" Vanna !" " Vanna !" " Van-
na !" and so on. MARCO *goes*
quickly to the steps which lead up
to the terrace.

It is Vanna! She comes — she is here!
They cry her name — they welcome her!
Hark! . . .

> [BORSO *and* TORELLO *follow him up*
> *on to the terrace, while* GUIDO *stands*
> *alone, leaning against a column, with*
> *a far-off look in his eyes. The*
> *noise without redoubles and comes*
> *nearer.* MARCO *looks down from the*
> *terrace.*

The squares, the streets, the byways are
full of heads and waving arms! The stones,
the very tiles of the roofs, are changed into
men! But where is Vanna? I see but a
cloud that parts a moment and closes again.
. . . Borso, my poor old eyes cheat my love.
. . . Age and tears and sorrow have blinded
them ; . . . they cannot find the only face they

seek. Where is she? Have you seen her?
Which way must I go to meet her?

BORSO

[*Restrains him.*] No, go not down. . . . The
multitude is too dense and cannot be held
back. They are crushing women, trampling
children under foot. And it is useless to go
—she will be here before you could reach
her. She draws nigh—yonder she is. She
lifts her head and sees us. . . . She quickens
her pace; . . . she looks up and smiles. . . .

MARCO

How is it you can see her and I not? Ah,
these failing eyes that can distinguish nothing clearly! For the first time I curse the old
age that has shown me so many things only
to hide this from me! But if you see her,
tell me—how looks she? Can you read her
face?

BORSO

She comes in triumph — the brightness
of her presence lights up the throng that
presses after her. . . .

[115]

TORELLO

But who is yonder man that walks at her side?

BORSO

I do not know him. . . . His face is hidden. . . .

MARCO

Hearken to the madness of their joy! All the palace trembles — the flowers fall from the great vases on the balustrade. The very stones quiver beneath our feet as they would rise and carry us away in this tumultuous gladness. . . . Ah! I begin to see. . . . The throng has reached the gates—it parts to one side and the other. . . .

BORSO

Ay, it parts to make room for her — to form a lane of triumph and of love through which she may pass. They shower upon her flowers and palms and jewels. . . . Women hold out their children to be touched by her; men stoop to kiss the stones her feet have pressed. Have a care—they come, and none can hold them! We shall be overthrown if

[116]

they mount the stairs. . . . Ah, the guards
rush in from every side to bar their passage.
. . . I will give order to drive them back and
close the gates, if it may yet be done. . . .

MARCO

Nay! Let the universal gladness have its
way here as in their hearts! It matters little
what is overthrown by it when their love
is so vast. They have suffered enough for
their deliverance to throw down every bar-
rier. My poor, dear people! I am carried
away and shout with you. . . . Oh, Vanna!
My Vanna! Is it you I see on the lowest
step? [*He moves to go and meet her, but*
Borso *and* Torello *hold him back*.] Hasten, hasten, Vanna! They will not let me
go to you! They fear the joy. . . . Come to
me, Vanna!—fairer than Judith and purer
than Lucrece! Come, Vanna!—come, mount
amid the flowers! . . . [*He runs to the great
vases of flowers and pulls handfuls of them,
which he throws down the stairs*.] I, too, have
flowers in honor of life—I, too, bring my lilies,
my laurels, and my roses to crown its glory!

[117]

[*The acclamations become wilder than ever.* VANNA, *accompanied by* PRINZIVALLE, *appears at the top of the staircase and throws herself into* MARCO'S *outstretched arms on the top step. The throng invades the staircase, the terrace, and the approaches, but keeps a certain distance from the group formed by* VANNA, PRINZIVALLE, MARCO, BORSO, *and* TORELLO.

VANNA

Father, I am so happy! . . .

MARCO

[*Embracing her closely.*] And I, my daughter, since I see you once more.   Let me look at you between our kisses. . . . You are more radiant than if you came from the farthest springs of that heaven that rejoices at your safe return. . . . The enemy has not robbed your eyes of a single ray of brightness nor your lips of one smile. . . .

VANNA

Father, I have much to tell you. . . . But
where is Guido?   Before all else I must set
him free from his torments. . . . He knows
not yet . . .

MARCO

Come, Vanna — yonder he stands. . . .
Come—I am thrust out, and it may be just-
ly; but there is pardon for your splendid
fault. . . . I must place you in his arms, that
my last act, my last glance, may find you in
the midst of love. . . .

> [*At this moment* GUIDO *advances tow-
> ards* VANNA. *She tries to speak, and
> moves as if to throw herself into his
> arms ; but he stops and repulses her
> with a harsh gesture ; then he speaks
> in an abrupt, strident, and imperi-
> ous voice to the others.*

GUIDO

Leave us!

VANNA

No, no!   Remain, all of you!   Guido, you
do not know. . . . I must tell you, I must tell

[119]

them all. Guido, I come back to you un-
sullied—no one can . . .

> [GUIDO *breaks in upon her words, his*
> *voice gradually rising with his anger.*

GUIDO

Come not near me—touch me not yet!
[*Advancing towards the crowd, which has begun to invade the hall, but retreats before him.*]
Did you not hear me? I have asked you
to depart and leave us alone. You are masters in your own houses—I am master here.
Borso and Torello, call the guards! Ah, I
read you well. You would have a spectacle
to crown your feast—but you shall not have
it. It is not for you—you are unworthy of
it. You have meat and wine—I have paid
for all; what more would you have? It is
the least you can do to leave me with my
grief. Go, eat and drink — I have other
cares, and I hold back the tears that you
shall not see. Go, I say! . . . [*The crowd
silently begins to thin out.*] Some of you still
linger? [*Takes his father roughly by the arm.*]
You, too—you, above all! More than all

the others, since it is through you that this has come. *You* shall not see me weep! I must be alone, alone as in the tomb, to learn that which I have to learn! [*Sees* PRINZIVALLE, *who has not moved.*] And you—who are you, that stand there like a veiled statue? Shame, that waits for me? Death, that waits for me? Know you not that you must go? [*Seizes a halberd from a guard.*] Must I drive you forth? Ha! you grasp your sword? I wear a sword, too; but I shall not use it for this. It is kept for one man—for him alone. . . . He, indeed. . . . But what are these veils that hide your face? I am in no humor for a masquerade. Wait, I will see who you are!

[*He approaches* PRINZIVALLE, *intending to uncover his face.* VANNA *throws herself between them.*

VANNA

Touch him not!

GUIDO

[*Stops, surprised.*] What, Vanna—**you?**
Whence is this force you put upon me?

VANNA

It is he that saved me. . . .

GUIDO

Saved you! Saved you, after—when it
was too late! In good sooth, a noble deed!
'Twould have been better done . . .

VANNA

[*With feverish eagerness*.] Let me speak at
last! Guido, I pray you! . . . One word, and
you will know. . . . He saved me, I tell you!
He spared me, reverenced me. . . . He did not
touch me. . . . He comes beneath my guardianship. I gave my word—our word. . . .
Wait till your anger . . . Let me speak to
you. . . . He said no word, lifted not a finger,
otherwise than . . .

GUIDO

But who is it? Who is it?

VANNA

Prinzivalle. . . .

GUIDO

Who—he? This man is Prinzivalle? . . .

[122]

VANNA

Yes, yes, ... he is your guest, ... he con-
fides in you! And he is our savior. ...

> [GUIDO *stands a moment as if stu-*
> *pefied, then begins to speak with*
> *an increasing violence and pas-*
> *sion that give* VANNA *no chance to*
> *interrupt him.*

GUIDO

What, my Vanna! Oh, this falls upon my
heart like a refreshing dew from the heaven
of heavens! Vanna! My Vanna! You are
great, and I love you. At last I understand!
Ay, you were right. ... Since it must be
done, this was the way to do it. At last I
see your wisdom, mightier than his crime!
I knew not, ... could not foresee. ...
Another would have killed him as did Judith with Holofernes; but his crime was
blacker, and called for a punishment more
dire. ... The manner of it was to lead him
hither as you have done, into the midst of
his victims, that shall be his executioners!
'Tis a splendid triumph! He followed after

your kisses, gently, meekly, as a lamb that
follows after a flowering bough. What
matter kisses given with hate behind? Behold him in the toils! Ay, you were right
—had you killed him there in his tent, after
his hideous crime, it would scarce have suf-
ficed; . . . there would have been a doubt
—none would have seen the deed. All the
world knew the abominable compact, and
it must likewise learn what it costs to outrage the nature of man so far. . . . How did
you gain it — the greatest triumph that a
woman's honor. . . . Ah, you shall tell
them! [*Strides to terrace and calls loudly.*]
Prinzivalle! Prinzivalle! We hold the foe!

VANNA

[*Clings to him and tries to restrain him.*]
No! no! Hearken to me! No, it is not as
you think. . . . Guido, I beg of you! . . . You
are wrong, Guido. . . .

GUIDO

[*Shakes her off and cries the louder.*] Un-
hand me!—you shall see! . . . [*To the multi-*

tude.] You may return—I bid you! And you, father, whose head peers between the balustrades as though to spy upon my fate, as though you waited for some god to descend and repair the evil you have done and bring back peace—you, too, shall return and gaze upon this peace and a mighty wonder! The very stones must see and hear that which is come to pass! I hide myself no longer, and my shame falls from me! I shall go hence purer than the pure—more joyous than those who have lost nothing. Now you may cry aloud my Vanna's name! And I cry with you, and louder than you all! [*Pushes into the hall those who appear on the terrace*.] Now shall you have indeed a spectacle! There is a justice in the universe. . . . Ah, I knew it—but I thought not it could be so swift! I looked to wait for it year after year. . . . I thought to watch for it in the forests, in the streets, at the corners of the lanes. . . . And now, lo! it stands before us, here in this hall! By what stupendous miracle . . . ? We shall know now—it is Vanna's work; since she is here, 'tis to ren-

der it complete. [*Takes* Marco *by the arm.*]
You see yonder man? . . .

MARCO

Ay. . . . Who is he?

GUIDO

You ask? Yet you have seen him, spoken
with him, been his easy messenger? . . .
[Prinzivalle *turns his head towards*
Marco, *who recognizes him.*

MARCO

Prinzivalle! . . .

[*Movement in the crowd.*

GUIDO

Ay, 'tis he — he, in truth — there is no
doubt. Approach and look upon him —
touch him — speak to him. Perchance he
has some new message? . . . Ah, it is no
longer the proud and splendid Prinzivalle—
but pity hath gone far from me. By a fiend-
ish and unheard-of plot he robbed me of the
one thing in the world that I held dear, the

[126]

one thing I could not give. . . . And, lo! he is
come hither, led by justice and by skill fairer
than justice, to seek of me the only recompense that I may give. Was I not right to
promise a miracle? Approach, have no fear
—he shall not escape us. . . . Yet close the
gates—no counter-miracle must snatch him
from us. We will not touch him for the moment—we will lengthen out our pleasures.
. . . My poor brothers, you whom he has so
tortured, you whom he would have massa-
cred, you whose wives and children he would
have sold for slaves, look upon him—this is
he; he is mine—he is yours, I tell you! But
he has not caused you to suffer like me—you
shall have him after I have had my fill. . . .
My Vanna brings him to us that our vengeance may wash out our shame! [*Speaking more directly to the crowd.*] Ye are all
here, and ye shall be witnesses—all must be
made plain. . . . Have you understood the
marvel? This man took Vanna for his own.
There was naught else to do—ye all willed it
so—and ye sold her. . . . I accuse none—
what is done is done; ye had the right to pre-

fer your lives to my poor happiness. But
how would ye have found the way to build
up love again with that which cast it down?
Ye knew but how to destroy—and there is
need to call to life! This hard thing Vanna
has done. She found a better deed to do
than Lucrece or Judith—the one slew herself, the other did to death the ravisher. . . .
Ah, that was too simple and too silent. Vanna slays not in a guarded tent—she brings to
us the living victim, that he may be slain in
the sight of all. We shall all join to efface the
infamy in which we all took part. . . . How
did she work this wonder, you ask? She shall
tell us. . . .

VANNA

Yes, I will tell you; but the thing is far
other than you think. . . .

GUIDO

[*Approaches her to kiss her.*] Let me kiss
you first, so that all may know—

VANNA

[*Repulses him vehemently.*] No, no, no—

not yet!   No, never again unless you listen
to me!   Hearken, Guido. . . . It is a question
now of an honor more real and a happiness
deeper than those that have driven you wild.
Ah! I rejoice that all my friends are here
once more.   They will hear me, perchance,
before you, understand me sooner than you
understand.   Hearken, Guido — I will not
come within your arms again until you
know. . . .

GUIDO

[*Still pressing her*.]   Soon enough I shall
know—but before all I would—

VANNA

Hear me, I say!   I have never lied—but
to-day, above all days, I tell the deepest
truth, the truth that can be told but once
and brings life or death. . . . Hearken, Guido, then — and look upon me, if you have
never known me until this hour, the first and
only hour when you have it in your power
to love me as I would be loved.   I speak in
the name of our life, of all that I am, of all
that you are to me. . . . Be strong enough to

9   [129]

believe that which is incredible. This man
has spared my honor. . . . He had all power
—I was given over to him. Yet he has not
touched me—I have issued from his tent as
I might from my brother's house.

GUIDO

Why?

VANNA

Because he loved me. . . .

GUIDO

Ah, that was what you were to tell us—
that was the miracle! Ay, already, at the
first words, I divined something beneath
them that I understood not. . . . It passed
me like a flash—I took no heed of it. . . .
But I see now that I must look more closely. [*Suddenly calmer.*] So, when he had
you in his tent, alone, with a cloak for
all your covering, all night long, you say
he spared you? . . .

VANNA

[*Vehemently.*] Even so!

[130]

GUIDO

He did not touch you, did not kiss you?

VANNA

I gave him one only kiss upon the brow—
and he gave it me again. . . .

GUIDO

On the brow! Look at me, Vanna. . . .
Am I a man to believe that the stars are
fragments of hellebore, or that one may drop
something into a well and put out the moon?
After what an adventure— Ah! I will not
say it—I would not ruin us beyond repair.
. . . I cannot see your purpose—or whether
it is the feverish madness of this night of
horrors that has unbalanced your reason—
or mine. . . .

VANNA

It is not madness—it is truth.

GUIDO

Truth! . . . Ah, that is all I seek! But
it must come with a face of human likeness.
What! a man desires you so utterly that he

will betray his country, stake all that he has
for one single night, ruin himself forever,
and do it basely, do such a deed as no man
ever thought to do before him, and make the
world uninhabitable to himself forever! And
this man has you there in his tent, alone and
defenceless, and he has but this single night
that he has bought at such a price—and he
contents himself with a kiss upon the brow,
and comes even hither to make us give him
credence! No, let us reason fairly and not
too long mock at misfortune. If he asked
but that, what need was there that he should
plunge a whole people into sadness, sink me
in an abyss of misery such that I have come
from it crushed and older by ten years? Ah!
had he craved but a kiss upon the brow, he
might have saved us without torturing us
so! He had but to come like a god to our
rescue. . . . But a kiss upon the brow is not
demanded and prepared for after his fashion. . . . The truth is found in our cries of
anguish and despair. . . . I judge not—it
is my own cause, and I see not clearly. . . .
Let others judge and answer for me! [*To*

the crowd.] You have heard. . . . I know
not why she speaks thus to us—but she has
spoken; and you shall judge. You ought to
believe her, because she has saved you!
Tell me, can you do it? Let all those who
believe her issue from the throng and stand
forth to give the lie to human reason! I
would see them and know what such men
are like!

> [MARCO *stands forth alone from the
> crowd; among the others, only timid,
> indistinct murmurs are heard.*

MARCO

[*Strides to centre.*] I believe her!

GUIDO

You are their accomplice! But the
others—the others! Where are they that
believe her? [*To* VANNA.] Do you hear
them? Those whom you have saved shrink
back at the thought of the laughter that
should fill the hall—they murmur, and
dare not show themselves. And I—I
ought—

VANNA

They are not bound to believe me—but
you, since you love me—

GUIDO

I, since I love you, must be your dupe!
Nay, listen to me. . . . My voice is not the
same—my wrath has died down. . . . These
things break a man's strength—I am becoming like a graybeard. . . . It is old age and
weakness of mind that shall take the place
of my anger that is gone from me. . . . I do
not know. . . . I seek, I grope with trembling
fingers to close them upon what remains of
my poor happiness. . . . I have no more but a
hope, so frail that I have not the heart to
strangle it. A word shall kill it—and yet
my anguish must hazard that word. Vanna,
I was wrong not to think of this throng when
I asked you. . . . I forgot your shamefaced-
ness that could not speak out. . . .You could
not tell them what the monster did. . . . Ay,
the question should have waited till we were
alone—then you would have avowed the
horrible truth. . . . But I know it, alas! too

well—and these others know it. . . . Why
seek to hide it, Vanna? It is too late. Now
there is no choice — shame must triumph
over itself. You will not think ill of me—
you will understand. . . . At such times reason knows no longer—

VANNA

Look in my eyes, Guido! In their gaze I
place all my strength, all my faithfulness, all
that I owe you for the last time. It is not
shame that speaks—it is the truth. This
man touched me not.

GUIDO

Good—excellently good. . . . There is no
more to say. . . . Now I know all. Yes, it is
the truth—or rather it is love! I understand. . . . You have wished to save him. . . .
I know not what a single night can have
wrought in the woman I loved so much. . . .
But this was not the way to save him. . . .
[*Raises his voice.*] Hear me, all of you, for
the last time! I am about to make an oath.
I cling a moment yet on the very brink of a

bottomless abyss—soon my hands will lose
their hold. . . . I would not ruin her. . . . Do
you hear me? My voice has lost its vigor.
. . . Draw nearer yet. . . . Ye see this woman—this man? It is assured that they love
each other. . . . Do not forget—I weigh each
word as they measure out a remedy, drop by
drop, at the bedside of a dying man. . . .
They shall go hence by my consent, freely,
with no outrage, without harm—they shall
carry with them all that they desire. Make
a path before them if you choose, and sprin-
kle it with flowers. . . . They shall go wherever love may guide their footsteps—only so
that this woman tell me the truth which is
the only possible one, the only thing that I
still love in her, and that she owes me for
what I give her. . . . You hear me, Vanna?
Answer me—did this man have your honor?
Yes or no—one word! That is all I ask. It
is neither a judgment nor a trap—I have
taken my oath, and all are witnesses. . . .

VANNA

I spoke the truth. . . . He touched me not.

GUIDO

Good—you have spoken—you have condemned him. There is no more to do. Now I rouse myself. . . . [*Turns to the guards and points to* PRINZIVALLE.] This man is *mine!* Take him, bind him, go down with him into the uttermost dungeons that lie beneath us. I go with you. [*To* VANNA.] You shall see him no more. Soon I shall return to tell you the real truth that his last words shall reveal to me. . . .

VANNA

[*Rushes among the guards, who seize* PRINZIVALLE.] No! No! He is mine! I have lied! I have lied! He forced me. . . . [*Thrusts the guards away.*] Stand aside— do not take my part! He is mine alone. My hands shall— Ah, cowardly, basely, he humbled me!

PRINZIVALLE

[*Struggling to control his voice.*] She lies—she lies to save me, but no torture—

VANNA

Silence! [*Turns to the people.*] He is afraid!
[*Approaching* PRINZIVALLE, *as though to bind
his hands.*] Give me the cords—give me
the chains, the irons! Now that my hate
hath found a voice at last, it is I that
shall hold him fast, I that shall deliver him
up! [*In a low voice to* PRINZIVALLE, *while
she fastens his hands.*] Not a word! He
saves us—he unites us! I am yours—I love
you! Let me bind you—be sure that I shall
deliver you. I shall be your keeper. We
will flee. . . . [*Cries loudly, as if to force him to
silence.*] Silence! [*To the crowd.*] He begs
for mercy under his breath! [*Discovers his
face.*] Look upon that face! It still bears
the traces of this night of horror! [*Turns
back her cloak on her blood-stained shoulder.*]
And I bear them likewise! Oh, this fearful
night of love! . . . Look upon him — this is
the man — hateful and cowardly! [*The
guards move as if to lead him off.*] No, no—
leave him to me! He is my victim—he is
my prey! I will have him for myself! Hold
him fast—you see he would fain escape!

[138]

GUIDO

Why came he hither? And you—why did
you lie?

VANNA

[*Hesitating, seeking for words.*] I lied. . . .
I know not. . . . I would not say. . . . Listen,
it is now that— Yes, you shall understand.
. . . One does not know, nor think, before-
hand. . . . When I went there, I did not
think. . . . But what is to be— Yes, you
shall know all—to your sorrow—but you have
willed it so. . . . Ah, I feared you—I went in
fear of love and its despair. . . . Now, since
you will it — good — I will tell you. [*In a
calmer and more assured voice.*] No, no, I
had not the thought you spoke of—I did not
bring him to his executioners to avenge us
both. The thought I followed was not so
glorious, but held more of love for you. I
thought to bring him to a cruel death—but
I desired also that the memory of this hideous night should not weigh upon you to the
end of our days. I would have avenged
myself alone, in the darkness—I would have
done him to death, slowly—you can see how

—little by little, until his blood, falling drop by drop, had washed out his crime. You would never have known the hateful truth; and the terrible remembrance would not have risen to check our dearest kisses. I feared that when you saw that image you could no longer love me. I was mad, I know—I asked too much. I longed for the impossible. But you shall know all.... [*Addressing the crowd*.] Since we have come thus far, and it is too late to spare our love, all must be understood. I will confess, and you shall be my judges. This is what I did. ... Yonder man used me even as I said, basely, cowardly. . . . I longed to slay him, and we struggled. ... But he disarmed me. ... Then I had a vision of a deeper vengeance, and I smiled upon him. He trusted to my smiles —ah! what fools men are! It is just to deceive them, since they worship falsehood. When one shows them life, they take it for death—when one offers them death, they grasp at it for life! He thought to master me, and I have mastered him! Behold him already in his tomb—and I shall put the

seals upon it! I brought him hither, deck-
ing him with kisses as a lamb with garlands
—and he is in my hands, that shall never
loose their hold! Ah, my fair lover Prinzivalle, we shall have kisses such as none
have ever known!

GUIDO

[*Approaches her.*] Vanna! . . .

VANNA

Come close and look at him! He was full
of hope—he believed me when I said I loved
him! He would have followed me to the
uttermost hell! Thus I kissed him. . . .
[*Kisses* PRINZIVALLE *ardently.*] Gianello, I
love you! Kiss me again! These are the
kisses that avail. . . . [*Turning to* GUIDO.]
He returns them even now! Ah, laughter is
too near such horrors. . . . Now he is mine—
mine before God and the world! I will have
him! It is the price of my night—a splendid
price! . . . [*She staggers and leans against a
pillar.*] Have a care. . . . I shall fall. . . . I
am too full of joy! [*Breathing with diffi-*

culty.]   Father, I give him into your charge
until my strength—   Let them lead him off
before—   Let them find a dungeon so deep
that no one shall be able—   And I will have
the key—I will have the key!   At once—do
you hear?   He is mine—my recompense—
and I will have him all my own. . . . Let no
man touch him. . . . Guido, he is mine!
[*Takes a step towards* Marco.]   Father, he
is mine—you will answer for him to me.
[*Looks fixedly at* Marco.]   You understand,
father?   You are his guardian — let not a
shadow of harm fall upon his face—let him
be given into my hands as he is now!
[*They lead* Prinzivalle *off*.]   Farewell, my
Prinzivalle!   Ah, we shall meet again!

> [Guido *is in the midst of the sol-*
> *diers,* who lead him roughly away.
> Vanna *utters a cry, and falls into*
> *the arms of* Marco, *who darts for-*
> *ward to catch her.*

MARCO

[*In a low voice, bending over her.*]   Yes,
Vanna, I understand—I see the meaning of

your lie. . . . You have achieved the impossible. . . . It was at once just and most unjust,
like all that men do. . . . And life is right. . . .
Calm yourself, Vanna—there will be need of
more lies, since we are not believed. . . . [*To*
GUIDO.] Guido, she calls you. . . . Guido,
she is coming to herself. . . .

GUIDO

[*Steps quickly forward.*] My Vanna! . . .
[*Takes her in his arms.*] She smiles. . . . My
Vanna, speak to me! I never doubted
you. . . . It is all over now—all shall be
forgotten in our splendid vengeance. . . .
'Twas but an evil dream. . . .

VANNA

[*Opens her eyes; in a feeble voice.*] Where
is he? . . . Ay, I know. . . . But give me
the key—the key of his prison. . . . No
other hand must—

GUIDO

The guards are coming—they will give it
you.

VANNA

I must have it alone, that I may be sure
—that no one else— It was, indeed, an evil
dream, . . . but a fairer one begins. . . . Ah!
a fairer one begins. . . .

CURTAIN